THE WORLD'S
SNIPING RIFLES

WITH
SIGHTING SYSTEMS AND AMMUNITION

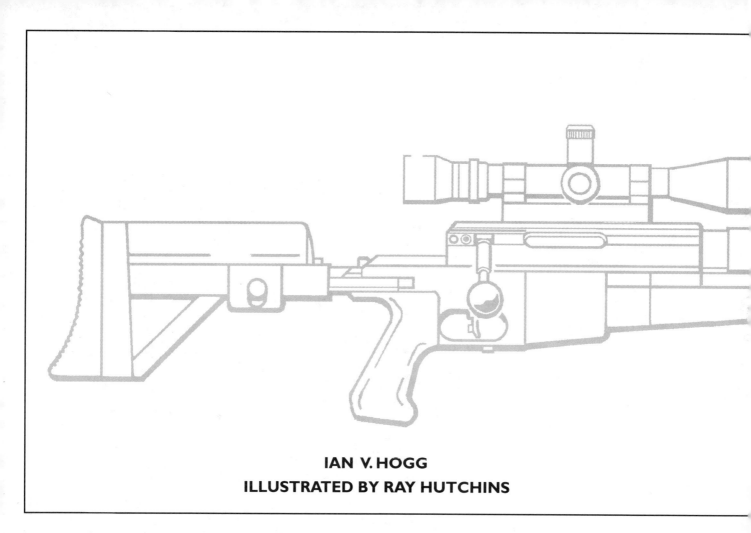

IAN V. HOGG

ILLUSTRATED BY RAY HUTCHINS

THE WORLD'S
SNIPING RIFLES
WITH
SIGHTING SYSTEMS AND AMMUNITION

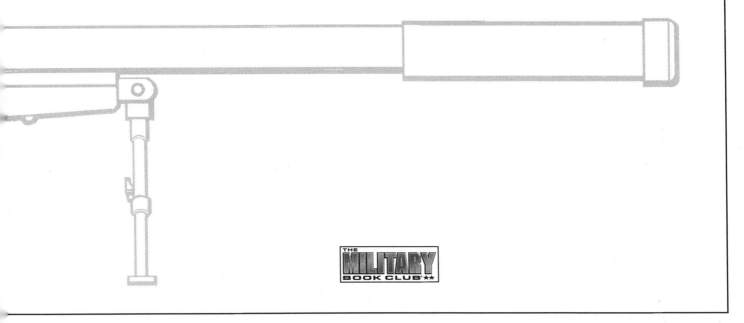

THE MILITARY BOOK CLUB ★★

**This book club edition is manufactured under license
from Greenhill Books / Lionel Leventhal Limited,
London.**

ISBN 1-85367-308-0

Typeset by Merlin Publications

INTRODUCTION

The snipe *(Gallinago gallinago)* is a small and very agile bird which spends its winters on English and Scottish marshes and its summers in Scandinavia. About ten inches long, with mottled black and brown plumage, it is an exceptionally difficult target for sport shooters, and was generally considered to be the ultimate test of a marksman. If you could hit snipe, you could hit anything. As a result, some time in the late nineteenth century, when sharpshooting became commonplace, some unknown British officer referred to it as 'Snipe shooting'. From that it became 'sniping'. Some claim that the expression can be found even earlier among the British in India, and though the bird does not appear to have ever visited that country, it is not beyond the bounds of possibility.

The shoulder-fired rifled firearm was invented some time in the 16th century in an attempt to produce an arm of better accuracy than the contemporary smoothbore arquebus. The idea succeeded, so much so that by 1550 the Swiss had rules which handicapped rifle shooters in competitions with smoothbore shooters and archers. But the rifle was an expensive and delicate instrument, used only for target and game shooting; it was not a weapon to be put into the hands of soldiers until it became much less expensive and much more robust.

This stage was reached in the 18th century, and the rifle first began to make itself felt in the American Revolution, or War of Independence, 1775 to 1783.

The settlers in America had brought with them gunmaking skills, and, since accuracy was a necessity of life, for both self-defence and self-sufficiency, rifles became relatively commonplace. And in the course of the revolution, the settlers used them to good effect against the British soldiers who, armed with the Brown Bess musket, were outshot both for range and accuracy. Not to be outdone, the British Army formed a corps of riflemen and even introduced the Ferguson breech-loading rifle into service in very limited numbers. The riflemen, principally armed with muzzle-loaders, began giving the settlers a taste of their own medicine, but by that time the war had been lost in effect, if not in legal fact, and they made little difference to the outcome.

Nevertheless, this campaign introduced the army to the idea of individual 'sharpshooters', clad in green clothing to blend in with their background, and operating independently to pick off individuals in the opposite ranks. The rifle regiment which had been formed was retained (and eventually became the 60th Regiment of Foot, and later the Rifle Brigade) and saw service in the Peninsular War

The Enfield 'Enforcer', a 7.62mm derivative of the Lee-Enfield rifle for police sniping, developed in the 1970s.

against the French where, once again, individual sharpshooters made their presence felt. But, it should be made clear, only as general sharpshooters against the enemy's outposts; on a few occasions when individuals had a French officer in their sights, they were smartly told to desist; officers were not there to be deliberately shot at by common soldiers. Such a procedure was almost tantamount to assassination, not the sort of thing to be permitted in honourable warfare.

No such inhibitions were put before the sharpshooters in the next major conflict, the American Civil War. Here the rifle came into its own and, fitted with primitive optical sighting telescopes, snipers were not only permitted to shoot at enemy officers, they were positively encouraged to do so. The first Union regiment of Sharpshooters was raised by Colonel Berdan in June 1861 and was armed with Colt revolving rifles, but these proving inefficient, they were replaced by Sharps' rifles in May 1862. Several regiments were raised, and were frequently clothed in green uniforms, but as well as acting as snipers they

A contemporary engraving of Berdan's Sharpshooters skirmishing in a cornfield during the American Civil War.

also formed skirmishing companies and performed reconnaissance tasks.

Confederate Sharpshooter battalions were also raised, but they tended to be employed as normal infantry when their sharpshooting abilities were not in demand, which appears to have been most of the time. The Confederates made the error of placing their sharpshooters in normal infantry brigade formations, which led to their being misemployed; the Union army kept them separate, as headquarters or corps troops, ensuring that they would be employed in the most effective manner according to the tactical picture of the moment.

The Franco-Prussian War of 1870-1 was the first war in which both sides were armed with breech-loading rifles as the primary infantry weapon, but it was a war of manoeuvre and encounter-battles and sharpshooting played no military part in it. Where such shooting did occur it was by *francs-tireurs*, the forerunners of guerrilla and partisan ambush warfare and was principally relatively short-range work. Many commentators have made much of the relative ranges of the Prussian Needle-gun (1700 yards) and the French Chassepot (2000 yards) but, as anyone who has ever fired a modern rifle at a man-sized target at even 1000 yards would admit, the prospect of deliberate hits at such ranges with those primitive rifles was remote in the extreme. That men were shot at extreme ranges is true, but this was the inevitable result of massed rifle fire; some of the bullets were bound to hit somebody.

It was the Boer War (1899-1902) which brought long-range accurate rifle shooting into prominence. This was not due to any superiority of the Boer's Mauser rifle over the British Lee-Metford; it was simply the natural result of the Boer farmer's upbringing. From an early age he was accustomed to shooting for his dinner, and ammunition was expensive, so he either became an efficient shot or went hungry. To a man accustomed to dropping a running antelope at 300 yards range, shooting a stationary man at 600 yards was child's play. The British soldier, on the other hand, was trained to deliver a devastating short-range fusillade against an attacking horde; and since the Boers chose not to attack in hordes, the British were thereby disadvantaged in the fire-fight.

This led, after the war, to a passion for long range shooting, even to a new design of rifle intended to deal out death and destruction at ranges well beyond that of the renowned Mauser, but it proved to be a totally impractical weapon and the British Army concentrated upon aimed rapid fire at normal fighting ranges, refusing to be lured away by the long-range mirage. As a Victorian expert had once said: *"The instruction of the British soldier in the use of an arm of precision must now be developed in proportion to the advantages which that arm is calculated to confer; and above all he must be taught that because he has a long-range rifle it is not necessary for him to employ it invariably at long ranges - that, as a general rule, it is undesirable that he should do so"*.

And so the British Army went to war in 1914 with a corps of infantry highly trained in combat musketry,

The sighting telescope on the standard British L42A1 Lee-Enfield sniping rifle.

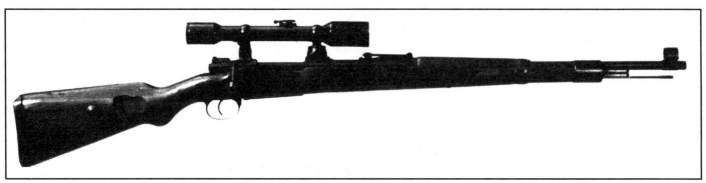

The German Army's standard sniping rifle in World War II was this Mauser Kar. 98k.

capable of loosing off up to thirty aimed shots a minute at ranges of up to about 300 yards with commendable accuracy. As events turned out, this was exactly the sort of rifle fire which was needed, and the 'Old Contemptibles', though seriously outnumbered, invariably gave the German Army a severe shock whenever it came too close. But once the mobile war came to a stop and the trench lines were dug, the nature of musketry took a different turn. Now it became a case of intermittent 'snap' shots at figures seen fleetingly on the other side of No Man's Land and, inevitably, some men were better at this than others, on both sides of the front. So these men gradually adopted the practice of lying concealed, waiting for the fleeting glimpse of a target silhouetted on the far side of a trench loophole or passing a damaged section of trench parapet. Whereupon the victim paid the price for his carelessness.

As with all armies, once private enterprise was shown to be profitable, it became institutionalised and official snipers were selected, sniping schools were begun, better rifles with better sights were provided and sniping became a commonplace fact of life on every front. Men vied for the job, for it gave them a far more independent life than simply standing in a trench waiting for the next attack or performing fatigues. The sniper, to a large degree, selected his own positions, went and came as he chose, and provided he was effective tended to be left alone to get on with it. But not every volunteer proved to be a success at this trade; it takes a special type of soldier to lie still and silent for hours, then fire a single shot, and continue to lie still and silent so as not to reveal his position by moving away. He also needed a certain amount of imagination so as not to immediately occupy the obvious bell-tower or lone tree which would be the focus of machine gun fire as soon as any sniper opened fire. He needed a great deal of fieldcraft and country lore to be able to move without attracting attention and conceal himself effectively, to understand the play of light and shade across the country, to estimate range and deflection.

After the war sniping became an almost forgotten skill; it was perhaps perpetuated in infantry schools, but the general line infantry was short of men and whilst it may have had room for a company sniper on the formal War Establishments he was rarely seen on the Peace Establishments. As a consequence, when World War Two broke out in 1939 there was a shortage of snipers in every army. As things turned out there was not much scope for snipers in the first years of the war; the confrontation of the Allied and German armies across the French frontier was conducted on a 'live and let live' basis, and when the Blitzkrieg struck in May 1940 events moved far too quickly for snipers to be tactically effective. Similarly the North African desert gave very little scope for sniping, and it was not until 1944, with the invasion of Europe, that the British found any scope for snipers. The Germans and Russians had found plenty of scope on the Eastern Front, however, and both sides had snipers working hard by 1942. The Americans encountered Japanese snipers in their island-hopping campaign in the South Pacific and soon developed their own sniping capability in order to counter the threat.

Generally speaking, the sniping rifles of World War Two were the service rifles, carefully selected for accuracy and provided with telescope sights. The British stuck to their Lee-Enfield, plus a number of Pattern '14 rifles specially adapted for sniping during World War One and brought back into service. The Germans used their stock Mauser Kar. 98k, the Russians their stock Mosin-Nagant 1891/30, both with the addition of telescopes, but the

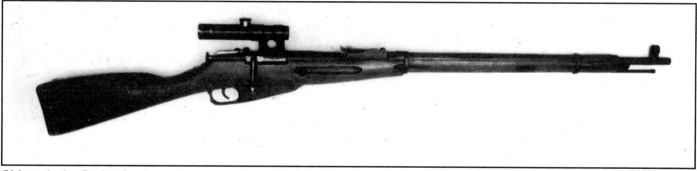

Although the Soviet Army used some semi-automatic rifles for sniping, most of their snipers relied on this bolt-action Mosin-Nagant Model 1891/30.

9

Russians also pioneered the use of a self-loading sniping rifle which did away with the often fatal movement of the sniper's hand and arm as he reloaded. The American army adopted the Garand semi-automatic in some cases, but the general preference was for the Springfield M1903, a special sniping version being developed.

World War Two saw a great deal of technical and scientific innovation, and among this was the adoption of infrared technology to permit locating targets in darkness. This was first thought of as a method of detecting aircraft, but the discovery of radar soon put infra-red out of business on that front. The Germans then developed it as a coast-watching device, with considerable success, and from there, as the technology improved and the equipment became more compact and reliable, as a night-driving aid. Then came an infra-red spotlight and an infra-red telescope which could both be attached to a rifle and, powered by a set of batteries carried in the man's pack, allowed shooting with accuracy out to about

A US Marine sniper team in Vietnam, using the Remington M40 rifle.

200 yards in pitch darkness. Similar development work had been done in Britain and the USA which resulted in British night-driving equipment and an American infra-red spotlight and telescope for night sniping. The latter equipment saw some use in the South Pacific theatre, but it was really more in the nature of an extended field trial than a practical aid to sniping. And it became apparent that with the range limited to 200 yards or so (by the

power available from a set of heavy batteries) it was more in the nature of a night sentry's device than a sniper's tool.

Sniping had its next outing in the Korean War; for this war there were still plenty of soldiers in the British and US armies with practical experience of sniping, and once the war settled down into the static phase around the 38th Parallel, sniping came into its own, though the equipment was still the same as that used in the 1939-45 war. There is a story told of an officer in the Commonwealth Division of the British Army who acquired a .50 Browning machine gun barrel, had a suitable bolt action and stock fitted by a Japanese gunsmith, and brought it across to Korea as a personal sniping tool. He was not popular with either side; them for being somewhat more than usually dangerous, and us for attracting retaliatory mortar fire.

Sniping then lay dormant, in the absence of any major conflict, for several years. But in the 1970s it suddenly began to attract a wider audience. This was the time of the terrorist, the hostage-taker, the

The German 'Vampir' infra-red night sight being tested by a British soldier in 1945. Note the size of the back-pack which contained batteries for the IR searchlight and compressed gas for cooling the IR detector in the sight unit.

hijacker and similar people. And when peaceful methods failed, it was soon seen that the solution lay in a sniper capable of taking action against the individual terrorist at long range and with surgical precision. Police and counter-terrorist forces thus began to appreciate the value of a trained marksman with a precision rifle, and rifle manufacturers were not slow to see the potential market.

Things now became technically interesting; in spite of various German and Russian semi-automatic rifles used for sniping in 1941-45, in the 1970s it was still generally accepted as Gospel that no semi-automatic rifle could ever be as accurate as a bolt-action weapon, and nobody outside the USSR would entertain such an idea. The Soviet Army had adopted the Dragunov in 1963, though this was not widely known in the west, and even then such knowledge would not have been accepted as a testimonial for the semi-automatic principle. The bolt-action reigned supreme. But during the 1980s improved semi-automatic rifles went into general service, and sniping versions began to appear.

By the late 1990s there is less resistance to the semi-automatic in the sniping role, but it takes an exceptional one to win a military contract; the bolt action is still dominant.

The other question which the 1975-90 period brought to the fore was the question of calibre and cartridge.

Service ammunition is built to a specification, and the accuracy element of that specification is somewhat below the standard which a sniper has the right to expect, and some manufacturers have said 'Never mind what the service standard is, our rifle is optimised to work with .243 Winchester (or some other cartridge) and that is our recommendation.''

The pages which follow exhibit the state of art as it stands in 1997, with details of sniping rifles in use around the world or which are currently being offered to the military and security markets. Most of these rifles are in production; a few are no longer produced, but remain in service and are likely to do so for some considerable time, since sniping rifles are slow to wear out. There are also pages of information on sighting systems and similar matters, since without sighting and target acquisition, even the best sniping rifle is at a disadvantage.

One of the first of the .50 specialist sniping rifles was this Model 500 from Research Armaments Industries of the USA.

The Future

Scarcely a year goes by without some advance in firearms design being announced, or so it seems to the casual observer. In fact many of these announcements are optimistic and vanish when more research is done; others are merely old ideas being given a new run because some aspect of technology has made them a little more attractive than they were in the past. But in all this activity, is there anything which promises improvements for the sniper?

Here, I think, we have to make a distinction between the two branches into which sniping has divided itself: anti-materiel and anti-personnel. The first thing to be realised about anti-materiel sniping is that, so far, many of its advantages are entirely theoretical; it has had very little trial in actual combat conditions, and the few trials it has had have not been very significant to the overall results of the operation. So whether the scenario of the infiltration party destroying a squadron of expensive jet fighters is a valid one, we have no way of knowing. So far as equipment goes the anti-materiel sniper is well provided with a variety of heavy calibre weapons, as the following pages show. But there are indications that enthusiastic designers are straying into the realms of giantism, and it cannot be long before somebody starts exploring the more powerful 20 mm and even larger cartridges, striving for the ultimate destructive power but with very little thought of the practicalities of carrying such monsters about the countryside. (Not to mention the weight of a reasonable quantity of ammunition.)

So far as anti-personnel sniping goes, we seem to have arrived at the same plateau of excellence that has already been reached with assault rifles; it might be possible to improve the performance, but by how much and at what sort of cost? "The final ten percent of performance is sixty percent of the development cost" say the guided missile engineers, and much the same is being said about more mundane weapons like rifles and machine guns. At the present, sniping rifles are generally so good that they are far more accurate than 99 out of 100 people can shoot them, and striving to make them any more accurate seems to be a waste of time and effort. Moreover it tends to price them out of the market; the prime example of this can be seen in the magnificent Walther WA2000 rifle which appeared in the mid-1980s. It was designed around the .300 Winchester Magnum cartridge, the barrel being dimensioned and rifled for that alone. The barrel was fitted into a frame so that the recoil force was in a straight line to the firer's shoulder, the gun was a gas-operated semi-automatic, it had every conceivable adjustment for length, height, fit, and trigger pull. It had a muzzle brake, recoil absorbers, a bipod, hand rests, a magnificent telescope sight. And it cost something in the region of $5000. By contrast, the current price of a top Parker-Hale rifle is just over $1000. As a result, Walther very wisely saw that there was no likelihood of a profit being made out of the limited number of weapons they were likely to sell and abandoned the WA2000 in 1988.

So I think we are likely to wait for some years before we see anything very startling appearing in the anti-personnel sniping field. And although we shall undoubtedly see some startling designs in the anti-materiel sniping field, whether they will meet with military acceptance is likely to wait until some practical experience is gained as to just what tactical function they really can perform, as opposed to the tactical functions they are expected to perform. Not for the first time, the development of a weapon system is going to have to wait until the military are satisfied that they can find a use for it.

CONTENTS

Steyr Anti-Materiel Rifle IWS 2000   Austria

In the late 1980s the **Steyr-Mannlicher** company took a long look at the targets which confronted the infantryman on the modern battlefield: men, helicopters, armoured personnel carriers, crew-served weapons, vehicles of all shapes and sizes, radar and similar surveillance and observation systems - the list appeared endless, and it was obvious that the ordinary rifle and machine gun could not hope to deal with all of them. From this, and spurred no doubt by the contemporaneous rise of the .50 rifle in the USA, Steyr set about 'Project 5075', the development of a heavy-calibre infantry weapon capable

of dealing with anything it met short of a main battle tank.

Two of the prime requirements were the ability to defeat hard targets and high velocity in order to produce a flat trajectory, with a consequent reduction in range errors. This led to the adoption of a fin-stabilised long rod projectile fired from a 14.5mm smooth-bore barrel at about 1400 metres per second. This demanded a substantial cartridge, and also a substantial weapon, and the design incorporated a take-down barrel so as to make it convenient for a two-man crew to carry, and a concentric recoil buffer and high efficiency muzzle brake to soak

up a large proportion of the recoil.

Initial firings with the first design proved that the design was sound; the tungsten dart could defeat 40mm of armour at 1000 metres range, and the highest point of the trajectory was only 800 mm above the line of sight at the same range. The rifle itself was a long-recoil operated semi-automatic, feeding from a five-shot side-mounted magazine.

Experience with this prototype led to some changes, notably raising the calibre to 15.2mm, and the project now became the 'Infantry Weapon System 2000'. Development is still being carried out, with a view to simplifying and lightening

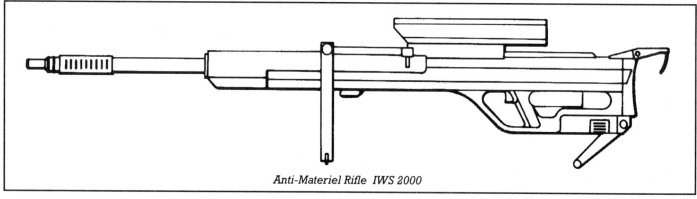

Anti-Materiel Rifle IWS 2000

the rifle, to producing a full-automatic version, and also to develop a rifled barrel version so as to allow a somewhat greater diversity of ammunition to be used.

The 15.2mm cartridge uses a composite metal/plastic case and is loaded with a 20 gram (0.71oz) tungsten dart. At 1000 metres this can deal with almost any target except a heavy tank, and against lighter targets it is effective out to 2000 metres. As might be expected, the standard sighting system for the rifle is a 10x telescope.

Right: *Assembling the IWS2000 rifle prior to firing.*
Below: *The Steyr IWS2000 anti-materiel rifle.*

Data:

Calibre: 15.2mm (0.598in)
Operation: Long recoil, semi-automatic
Length: 1800mm (70.86in)
Weight: 18kg (39.7lbs)
Barrel: 1200mm (47.25in), smoothbore
Magazine: 5 rounds, side-mounted
Muzzle velocity:
1450m/sec (4757ft/sec)

Manufacturer:
Steyr-Mannlicher, Steyr, Austria

Steyr Scharfschützen Gewehr 69   Austria

This rifle was designed in the 1960s in response to an Austrian Army requirement, and was adopted by that force as their **Scharfschützengewehr (SSG) 69**. It has remained in production ever since and numerous variations have been developed including a police version, a silenced version, a short-barrelled version and so on.

This was probably the first production rifle to use the cold-forging system developed by Steyr in which the barrel is formed by placing a hollow steel tube over a former which is shaped to the chamber and rifling, and then hammering it so that the metal flows and takes up the internal contours required as well as expanding to the desired length. This produces a barrel very close to the final dimensions, requiring little machining, and also work-hardens the metal to give the weapon a long accuracy life.

The bolt is locked by six rear lugs, and the magazine is a rotating spool type which has been in use in Mannlicher rifles since the 1890s. It holds five rounds and forms a very compact unit which can be removed from below the action. A transparent plastic cover at the rear end allows a quick check of the contents at any time. The original models were designed to accept, as an alternative, a conventional ten-shot box magazine, but this, over the years, appeared not to be wanted and was eventually dropped from the list of options.

The stock is of synthetic material. The receiver is formed with a top rib to which almost any type of sight can be attached. Iron sights are provided for emergency use, but normal shooting is always done with a telescope sight, the standard being the Kahles ZF69, with 6x magnification and internal adjustment to 800 metres range. At this range, using RWS Match ammunition, the rifle will put ten shots into a 400mm (15.7in) circle.

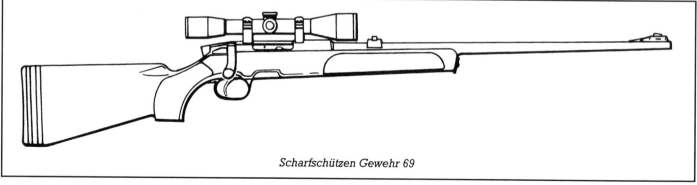

Scharfschützen Gewehr 69

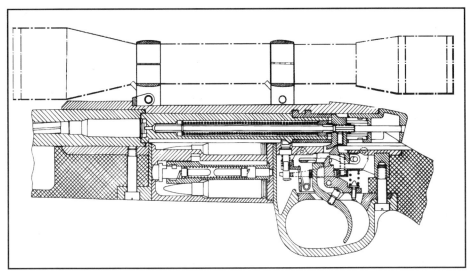

Above: The trigger, bolt and magazine mechanism of the SSG-69.

Below: The heavy-barrel 'Police' version of the SSG-69.

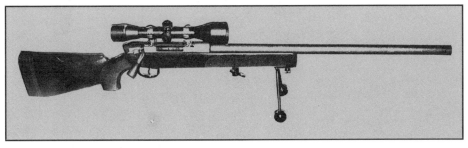

The Steyr SSG-69 fitted with silencer.

The Steyr-Mannlicher SSG-69 with synthetic stock and telescope sight.

Data:
Chambering: 7.62 x 51mm NATO or .243 Winchester
Operation: Bolt action
Length: 1140mm (44.9in)
Weight: 3.90kg (8.6lbs)
Barrel: 650mm (25.6in), 4 grooves, right-hand twist
Magazine: 5 rounds, rotary
Muzzle velocity: ca 860 m/sec (2820ft/sec)

Manufacturer:
Steyr-Mannlicher, Steyr, Austria

FN Model 30-11 Belgium

Fabrique Nationale d'Armes de Guerre of Herstal-lèz-Liége, Belgium, was set up in 1889 to make Mauser rifles, under license, for the Belgian Army. The company subsequently made something over one million rifles for Belgium and several other countries. In the 1920s FN developed a Mauser-style design of their own, widely sold as the FN Model 24, and this was revised slightly in 1930. Production of the Model 30 was resumed after World War Two, but by that time the demand for bolt-action rifles was dwindling, and with the company's successful FAL design of automatic rifle becoming the standard of some fifty armies, production of the Model 30 fell to almost nothing.

In the 1970s, however, FN saw that there was a demand for a robust and uncomplicated sniping rifle for police and security forces, and took the Model 30 as the basis for a precision rifle, the **Model 30-11.**

The **30-11** uses a standard Mauser 98 bolt action, with front and rear lugs, attached to a carefully-mounted heavy barrel. The trigger pull is set to 1.3kg (2.87lbs) but can be adjusted by the user around that figure. The stock is of wood, and the butt is adjustable for length and height by means of variously-sized inserts, so that virtually any size of firer can be accommodated. The bipod used is that of the FN-MAG general-purpose machine gun. A firing sling or hand-stop can also be attached under the fore-end if desired.

The standard rifle was equipped with

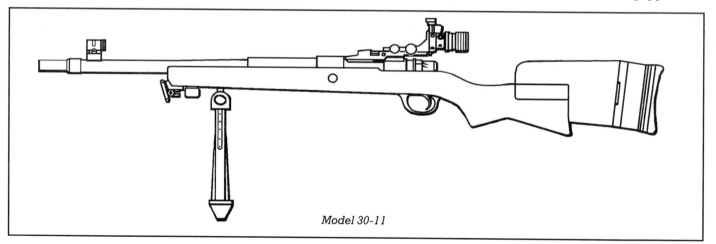

Model 30-11

a hooded foresight and an Anschütz adjustable dioptric rear sight. However, the rifle could also be supplied without iron sights and with a special mount and FN 4 x 28 telescope sight. Various types of adapter could be provided for fitting other telescopes or electro-optical sights.

The original production appears to have been in 7.92mm Mauser calibre, but this was soon changed to 7.62mm NATO chambering. Although the standard Mauser integral 5-round box magazine is usual, several rifles have been seen with 10-shot removable box magazines which could be provided as an option.

Manufacture of the **Model 30-11** ceased in the late 1980s, but several hundred were supplied to police forces and armies around the world and will be in service for several years to come.

The FN 30-11 sniping rifle with telescope sight.

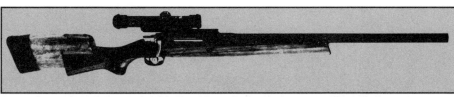

An early version of the model 30-11 without flash eliminator and iron sights.

Data:

Chambering: 7.62 x 51mm NATO
Operation: Bolt action repeater
Length: 1117mm (44 in)
Weight: 4.85kg (10.7 lbs)
Barrel: 502mm (19.75in),
4 grooves, rh, 1 turn in 305mm (12in)
Magazine: 5 shot integral or 10-shot removable box.
Muzzle velocity:
850 m/sec (2790 ft/sec)

Manufacturer:
FN Herstal SA, Liege, Belgium.

Sako TRG-21/41   Finland

Sako, who have been building rifles of all kinds for many years, remain firmly convinced that for accurate shooting the bolt action cannot be bettered, and they therefore developed their 'TRG Sharp-Shooting System' around a classical bolt action design. Two models are produced, identical except for calibre; the **TRG-21** fires the standard 7.62 x 51mm NATO cartridge, while the **TRG-41** fires the .338 Lapua Magnum round.

The heavy barrel is formed by the cold-hammering method, as is the receiver body. The barrel is fitted with a muzzle brake which also acts as a flash hider; a suppressor can be fitted on to the brake, which then forms part of the silencer. There is thus no need to remove the brake, as with most other silencer-fitted designs. The bolt has three lugs and a 60° lift, giving minimum bolt movement. An integral dovetail rail above the receiver will accept almost any kind of optical or electro-optical sight, and adjustable folding iron sights are provided for emergency use.

There is a two-stage trigger, which can be adjusted for pressure between 1 and 2.5kg (2.2 to 5.5lbs); it can also be adjusted for length and horizontal or vertical pitch to suit the firer's grip. The safety catch is located inside the trigger guard and is entirely silent in operation. Applying the safety locks the bolt and trigger, and also blocks the firing pin from the primer cap. The detachable box magazine holds ten rounds of 7.62mm or five rounds of .338 ammunition.

The stock is of synthetic material on an aluminium frame. The butt is capable of adjustment, using spacers, for length,

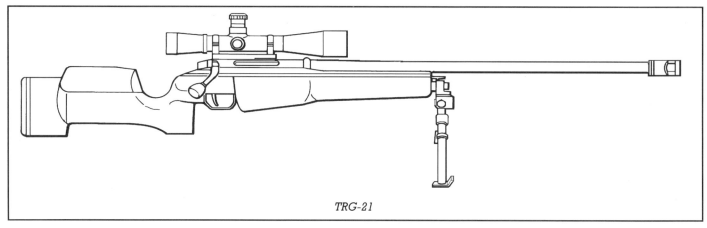

TRG-21

The Sako TRG-21 sniping rifle.

angle, height and pitch, and the cheek-piece is independently adjustable for height and pitch. The stock can be used equally well by left or right-handed firers, and the design allows the rifle to be used for sniping, international target shooting or military rapid-fire competitions.

Manufacturer:
Sako Ltd, Riihimäki, Finland

Data (TRG21):

Chambering:7.62x51mm NATO
Operation: Bolt action
Length: 1150mm (45.28in)
Weight: 4.7kg (10.36lbs)
Barrel: 660mm (26.0in), 4 grooves, right-hand twist, one turn in 280mm (11in).
Magazine: 10 rounds
Muzzle velocity:
ca 850 m/sec (2790ft/sec)

23

Sako SSR Mark 1   Finland

The Oy Vaimeninmetalli AB company of Finland have specialised for many years in the development and production of silencers for various types of firearms. As a result, when Sako decided that a silenced sniping rifle would be an asset, their obvious course was to collaborate with Vaime to develop a rifle and silencer perfectly matched to each other and 'all of a piece' instead of being a simple but cumbersome add-on device.

Sako are one of the firms who believe that precision and automatic rifles don't always go together, and that for the utmost perfection in sniping a bolt-action rifle is unquestionably the best answer. The result is this **SSR (Silenced Sniper Rifle) Mark 1** in 7.62mm NATO chambering. (There is also a Mark 3 model, chambered for the .22 Long Rifle rimfire cartridge and designed at the request of various European anti-terrorist and SWAT teams for short-range precision sniping in urban situations where penetration is to be avoided.)

The **SSR Mark 1** is generally similar to the Sako TRG-21 rifle as far as the action goes, a turn-bolt using triple locking lugs working in a cold-forged receiver. The stock is also very similar, with a pistol-grip contour and with all the requisite adjustments. The barrel, however, is formed into an integral silencing unit designed by Vaime.

The silencer/barrel configuration is

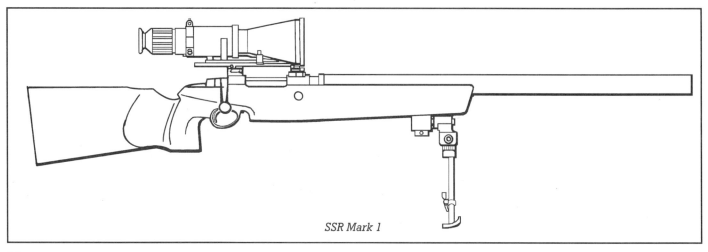

SSR Mark 1

designed to be at its most effective when using **Sako** sub-sonic ammunition. This has been specially loaded to develop the utmost possible accuracy combined with silent shooting. Due to the lowered velocity and the shorter effective length of barrel, the maximum range with this ammunition is 300 metres. For optimum accuracy 200 metres is preferred; at this range five-shot groups of 60mm (2.36in) or less are standard.

It is also possible to fire standard full-velocity ammunition from the rifle; this gives a better maximum range with a high degree of sound damping but, of course, the sonic boom of the bullet remains. This can, today, be a grave disadvantage in military sniping since electronic detectors which register this sonic wave and calculate the direction and range from which it was fired are now becoming available. Moreover, the psychological effect of a completely silent shot is much greater than that of a shot where the bullet noise is heard.

No iron sights are fitted; there is a NATO-standard mount for optical or electro-optical sights, and Sako provide a NATO-approved telescope sight which is graduated in metres to correspond with the trajectory of their sub-sonic ammunition.

The Sako SSR Mark 1 sniping rifle

Data:

Chambering: 7.62 x 51mm NATO (Sub-Sonic; see text)
Operation: Bolt action repeater
Length: 1180mm (46.46in)
Weight: 4.10kg (9.04lbs)
Barrel: 465mm (18.3in); silencer length 660mm (25.98in)
Magazine: 5 shot box
Muzzle velocity: ca 300 m/sec (985ft/sec)

Manufacturer:
Sako Ltd., Riihimäki, Finland

Rifle FR- F1 and FR-F2 France

When the French Army went looking for a sniping rifle in the 1960s, it demanded a bolt-action weapon; and since it already had a perfectly serviceable bolt action system in its now-obsolete MAS-36 rifle, it took it and built its sniping rifle around it. The result was the **FR-F1 (Fusil à Répétition, Modèle F1)**

The rifle has a longer barrel than the original MAS-36, giving more consistent ballistics and superb accuracy, and is half-stocked in wood. The butt is provided with spacers for adjusting the length, and there is also an adjustable cheek-piece. Iron sights, with luminous spots for firing in poor light, are fitted, but the normal sight is a Modèle 53bis telescope sight, which is carried in a special transit case and fitted to a mount on the rifle when required. It gives 4x magnification and can easily be adjusted so as to zero it to the rifle; once so adjusted it can be mounted and dismounted without affecting the zero.

The **F1** rifle was originally issued chambered for the standard 7.5 x 54mm French service cartridge, but when France aligned itself with NATO, the rifle was modified to chamber the 7.62 x 51mm NATO round. In both calibres the French Army was careful to provide match-grade ammunition for its snipers.

In 1984 a new version, the **FR-F2** appeared. This went into service alongside the **F1**; it did not replace it, but as the **F1** models wore out, they were replaced with **F2**s, and as a result there are still a number of **F1** models in use. The **F2** is basically the same rifle but with modifications which had suggested themselves during experience with the **F1**. The stock fore-end is now of steel,

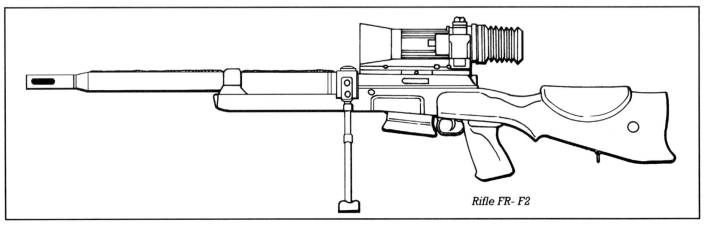

Rifle FR- F2

covered in matt black plastic. The bipod is stronger and has been moved back so that it can be more easily adjusted by the firer without too much movement. The most obvious change is the addition of a black plastic thermal sleeve around the barrel, which has three functions: 1) it prevents the heat of the sun, on a very hot day, warping the barrel; 2) it prevents a heat haze rising from a hot barrel and interfering with the sight line; and 3) it lessens the 'infra-red signature' of the weapon and makes it less likely to be detected.

The **FR-F2** is chambered only for the 7.62 x 51mm NATO cartridge; it uses the same sights and is similar in all dimensions to the **F1**.

Export versions of the **F2**, known as the FR-G1 and FR-G2 exist; they use a wooden fore-end and do not have the thermal sleeve; they differ in that the G1 has a non-adjustable fixed-length bipod, while the G2 has an adjustable and articulated bipod.

Breech and sights of the FR-F1; note the rubber cap on the base of the magazine which can be removed and used to close the magazine mouth against dirt when it is removed from the rifle.

The French FR-F1 sniping rifle in use.

Data:

Chambering: 7.62 x 51mm NATO or 7.5 x 54mm French Service
Operation: Bolt action
Length: 1138mm (44.8in)
Weight: 5.20kg (11.46lbs)
Barrel: 552mm (21.73in), 4 grooves, right-hand twist,
one turn in 305mm (12in).
Magazine: 10 rounds
Muzzle velocity:
ca 850 m/sec (2790ft/sec)

Manufacturer:
Giat Industries, Versailles-Satory, France

Firing the French FR-F2

Opposite top: *The French FR-F2 ready for action.*

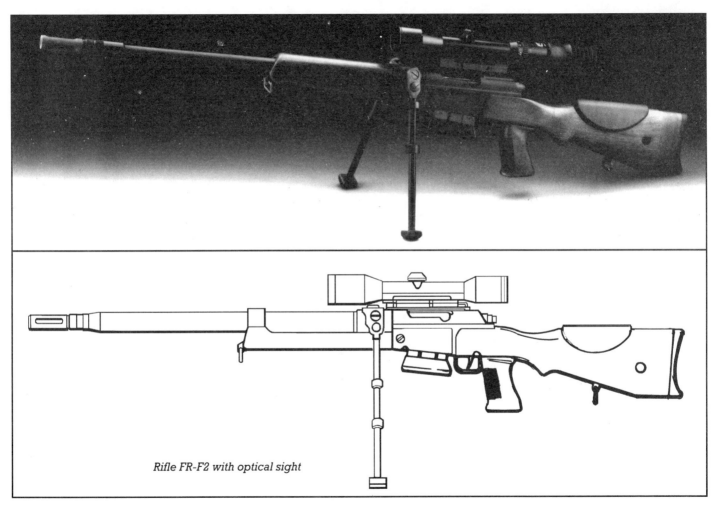

Rifle FR-F2 with optical sight

PGM Model UR Intervention France

The letters 'UR' stand for 'Ultima Ratio', the 'Last Argument', and are the trademark associated with this French company. They have made target rifles for a number of years, and in the late 1980s began producing highly specialised sniping rifles for police and military use. This 'Intervention' model is the basic model of the UR range.

Like all PGM rifles, the 'Intervention' is built on a modular system, with all the component parts mounted on a central rigid metallic girder made of aircraft quality alloy. The heavy, free-floating barrel is deeply fluted so as to disperse heat rapidly, and has an integral muzzle brake. The barrel is quickly interchangeable for a silenced barrel or for the barrel of any other 'UR' rifle of the same calibre, and removing and replacing the barrel does not upset the zero. The bolt has three locking lugs and an oversized knob. The shoulder stock is fully adjustable, allowing optimum shooting comfort, and the bipod, attached to the fore-end, is fitted with an axial brake which prevents accidental tilting and allows adjustment to any sort of terrain.

The trigger mechanism is a two-stage military type, with distinct first and second pressures, but built to match quality for a precise and repeatable release. No sights are fitted, but the rifle is fitted with a dovetail rail to attach Universal, Weaver or NATO-Standard telescope mounts, or commercial 25mm or 30mm ring mounts.

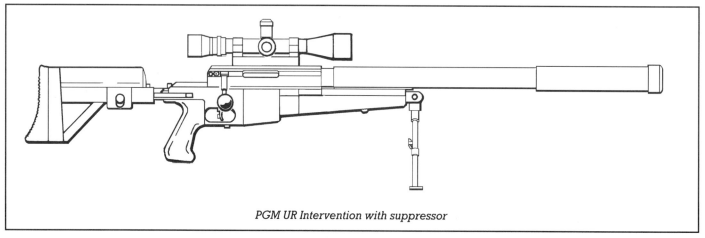

PGM UR Intervention with suppressor

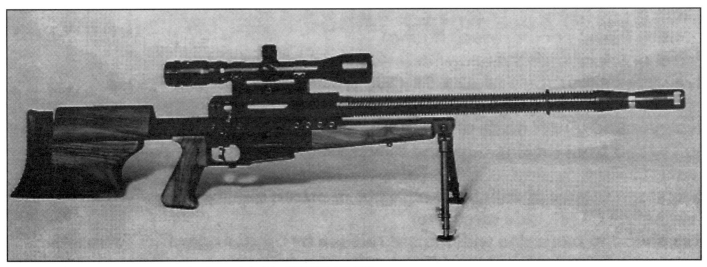

The 'Ultima Ratio Intervention'; the basic model of the 'ULTIMA RATIO' weapons range.

Tests with the silenced barrel show a reduction in noise, measured at 5 metres from the muzzle, from 113 decibels to 83; by way of comparison, an air pistol produced 71dB under the same conditions. And at 100 metres, with the standard barrel, the rifle will put five shots into a 19mm (0.75in) circle.

Data:

Chambering: 7.62 x 51mm NATO and others
Operation: Bolt action
Length: 1030mm (40.55in)
Weight: 5.50kg (12.12lbs)
Barrel: 600mm (23.62in)
Magazine: 5-round detachable box
Muzzle velocity:
305 m/sec (1000 ft/sec)

Manufacturer:
PGM Précision, Les Chavannes, France

PGM Model UR Commando

France

There are two models in the PGM **UR 'Commando'** range; the **'Commando I'** has a fixed stock, and the **'Commando II'** has a folding stock.

The **'Commando I'** is very similar to the UR 'Intervention' model described previously, differing principally in having a shorter barrel. It uses the same modular method of construction in which all the component parts are attached to a central rigid 'skeleton' girder of aluminium alloy, and also has the same quick-change barrel attachment which permits the standard 470mm (18.5in) barrel to be removed and replaced by either the longer 600mm (23.6in) 'Intervention' barrel or the silenced barrel. Changing the barrel is done very easily, the only tool required being a 5mm Allen key. It will be noted that the 'Commando' models use a slightly different design of muzzle brake, necessary because of the shorter barrel.

The folding stock of the **'Commando II'** model swings to the left and forward so that the folded weapon can be fitted into standard airborne troop packs. When unfolded, the locking catch has automatic compensation for the unlatching clearance so that the stock is absolutely rigid in use.

As with other models, the **'Commando'** series does not have iron sights, but the rifle is fitted with a dovetail rail accepting Universal, Weaver or NATO-standard sight mounts, or, alternatively, with commercial 25mm or 30mm ring mounts.

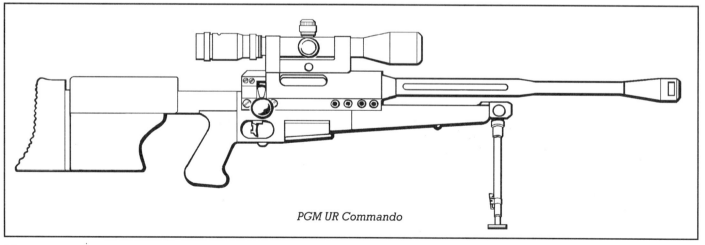

PGM UR Commando

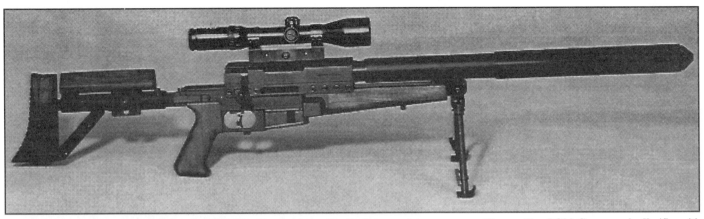

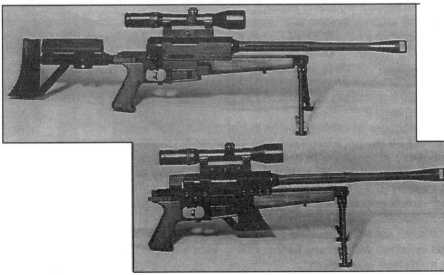

Above: *The PGM Commando II rifle with silencer barrel fitted.*

Left: *The PGM Commando II with butt extended and butt folded.*

Data:

Chambering: 7.62 x 51mm NATO and others
Operation: Bolt action
Length: 1020mm (40.15in); (740mm [29.13in] with stock folded)
Weight: 5.50kg (12.12lbs)
Barrel: 470mm (18.5in)
Magazine: 5 rounds
Muzzle velocity:
ca 290 m/sec (950 ft/sec)

Manufacturer:
PGM Précision, Les Chavannes, France

PGM Model UR Hecate   France

The UR 'Hecate' is the largest rifle in the PGM UR range and has been designed around the .50 Browning machine gun cartridge. Its purpose is interdiction and demolition shooting at long ranges, harassing fire and counter-sniping, and also the destruction of explosive ordnance (unexploded bombs or sea mines, for example) at a safe distance.

The 'Hecate' uses a similar modular construction to the smaller-calibre PGM rifles, basing the various parts on a high-grade aluminium alloy 'backbone'. The receiver is of high grade steel, and the barrel and stock are attached to it. The barrel is deeply fluted in order to disperse heat, and is fitted with an extremely high efficiency muzzle brake which reduces the felt recoil to about the level expected of a 7.62 x 51mm cartridge. The manual bolt uses three massive front lugs, and a very light firing pin ensures a short lock time. A two-stage military trigger is fitted but is carefully designed to provide a distinct and repeatable let-off point.

With a maximum accurate range in excess of 1500 metres (1640 yards), no iron sights are fitted, and the receiver is formed into a dovetail which will accept Universal, Weaver or NATO-STANAG mounts without further fitting. Optical or electro-optical sights of any type can thus be utilised.

The bipod is attached so that its centre of rotation is the barrel axis, and it is fitted

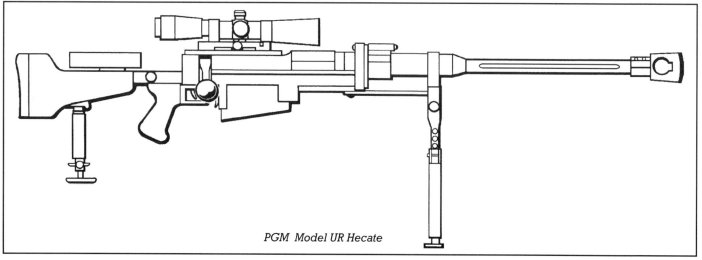

PGM Model UR Hecate

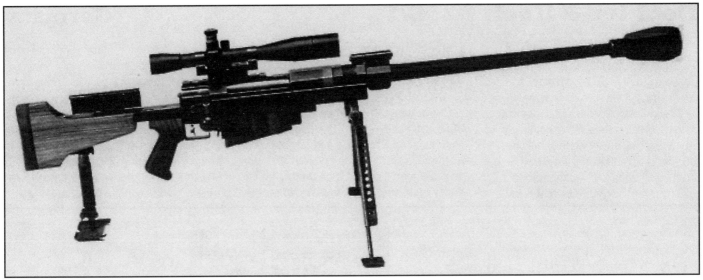

The PGM 'Hecate' 12.7mm anti-materiel rifle

with an axial brake to prevent accidental tilting. There is also a monopod to support the butt for long periods and thus relieve the firer of strain. For easy transport in the field, the stock can be quickly removed and there is a collapsible carrying handle at the centre of balance of the remaining mass.

Any type of .50 Browning (12.7 x 99mm) ammunition can be used, but the ultimate accuracy will be obtained by using hand-loaded ball ammunition; service machine gun ball is not usually manufactured to a fine enough tolerance for sniping, although it may be acceptable for firing at large material targets; when special bullets (AP or incendiary) are necessary for the desired terminal effect, there will, of course, be no choice but to use stock machine gun ammunition.

Data:

Chambering: 12.7 x 99mm Browning
Operation: Bolt action
Length: 1380mm (54.33in)
Weight: 13.80kg (30.42lbs)
Barrel: 700mm (27.56in)
Magazine: 7 rounds
Muzzle velocity:
ca 825 m/sec (2705 ft/sec)

Manufacturer:
PGM Précision, Les Chavannes, France

Heckler & Koch G3SG/1

Germany

The Heckler & Koch G3 is the standard German Army rifle; the **G3SG/1** is the sniping (SG-Scharfschützen Gewehr) variation and is widely used by German police and special forces and also by the Italian Carabinieri.

During manufacturing inspection the standard G3 rifles are fired under strict conditions to check their accuracy and consistency. Those which are particularly good in delivering tight groups of shots are put to one side for further examination, and if they live up to their promise by repeating their performance they are then modified into sniping rifles. Firstly the trigger mechanism is removed and replaced by a special set trigger unit which can have its pull-off adjusted. Once the trigger is set (which can only be done when the fire selector switch is in the single-shot position) it needs only a light touch to fire the rifle; the exact amount of pressure can be set between 900 and 1500 grams (approximately 2 to 3.3lbs). To 'un-set' the trigger, all that needs doing is to move the selector switch off the single-shot mark. Having fired with the set trigger, unless it is manually re-set, the next round will be fired at the

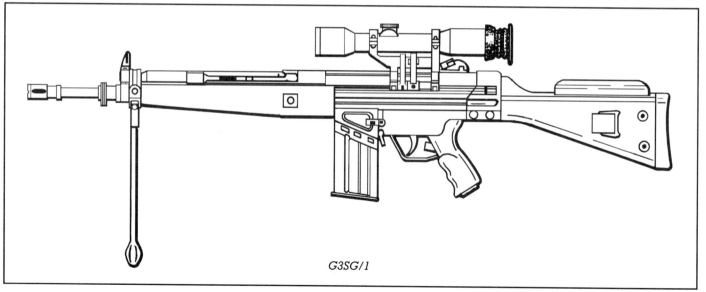

G3SG/1

normal pressure, which in this rifle is 2.6kg (5.7 lbs).

The standard iron sights remain on the rifle but it is now fitted with a telescope mount. The rifle is normally supplied with a telescope sight made by Schmidt & Bender or by Zeiss, a zoom telescope allowing 1.5x to 6x magnification and with range markers to 600 metres. The aiming graticule is divided into mil divisions, which allows the firer to move his shots a precise distance, provided he knows the range, or allows him to obtain the range provided he can estimate the size of some object in the field of view and close to the target.

Above: *Heckler & Koch G3SG/1 sniping rifle, left side*

Below: *Heckler & Koch G3SG/1 sniping rifle, right side*

Data:

Chambering: 7.62 x 51mm NATO
Operation: Semi-automatic, roller-delayed blowback
Length: 1025mm (40.35in)
Weight: 5.54kg (12.21 lbs)
Barrel:
450mm (17.7in), 4 grooves, right-hand twist, one turn in 305mm (12in).
Magazine: 20 rounds
Muzzle velocity: ca 800 m/sec (2625 ft/sec)

Manufacturer:
Heckler & Koch GmbH, Oberndorf/Neckar, Germany

Heckler & Koch G8   Germany

The **Heckler & Koch G8** rifle is an unusual attempt to provide an all-purpose weapon, and it is even more unusual in succeeding. In its basic form it is a selective-fire rifle, with a heavy, removable barrel; it is this heavy barrel which allows it to be used as a sniping rifle when the need arises, for it delivers more than adequate accuracy and consistency out to medium ranges. However, it is also capable of automatic fire; when this option is selected, the normal box magazine can be replaced by a 50-round drum magazine which feeds into the normal magazine housing. And since a hot barrel can be quickly removed and exchanged for a cool one, it is possible to use the **G8** as a support machine gun; since this will demand a fairly generous ammunition supply, it is possible to remove the magazine housing and replace it with a belt-feed unit to permit the use of 250-round belts. The final option is the ability to fire three-round bursts for a single pressure on the trigger.

With all these options combined into one weapon, it is not surprising that the **G8** has been widely adopted by German and other European police forces. In one weapon, complete with its accessories, they have a sniping rifle, an assault rifle, and a tactical machine gun. Not surprisingly, various other uses have been seen, and at least one manufacturer has produced a grenade-launching attachment which allows standard tear-gas and smoke grenades to be fired to ranges of up to 150 metres.

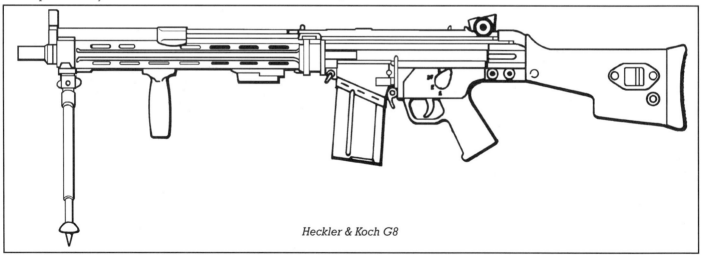

Heckler & Koch G8

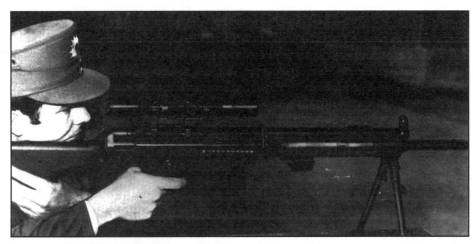

Above: The Heckler & Koch G8 in use as a sniping rifle.

Left: 50-round drum magazine for the G8 rifle

Above right: The Heckler & Koch G8 rifle with accessories: drum magazine, front grip, spare barrel, belt-feed kit and sling.

Data:

Chambering: 7.62 x 51mm NATO
Operation: Selective-fire automatic, roller-delayed blowback
Length: 1030mm   (40.55in)
Weight: 8.15kg (17.97lbs)
Barrel: 450mm (17.7in), 4 grooves, right-hand twist, one turn in 305mm
Magazine: 20 round box; 50 round drum; 250 round belt.
Muzzle velocity:
835 m/sec (2740 ft/sec)

Manufacturer:
Heckler & Koch GmbH,
Oberndorf/Neckar, Germany

Heckler & Koch HK33-SG1   Germany

The **HK33** rifle was developed as the 5.56mm calibre version of the standard H&K G3. It was developed in the 1970s and was one of the first European designs in this calibre; it has been adopted as a service rifle by several armies worldwide. Following the incorporation of Heckler & Koch into the Royal Ordnance organisation, production of this rifle is now concentrated in Britain, at the Nottingham factory of RO.

The **SG1** is the sniping version and, like the G3SG/1 (q.v.), is arrived at by selecting the best of the production rifles and then reassembling it with extra care and providing it with an improved trigger system. As with all the HK designs, the mechanism is delayed blowback, using a roller-delayed bolt which is in two parts. On firing, the lighter front section is driven back by the gas pressure in the

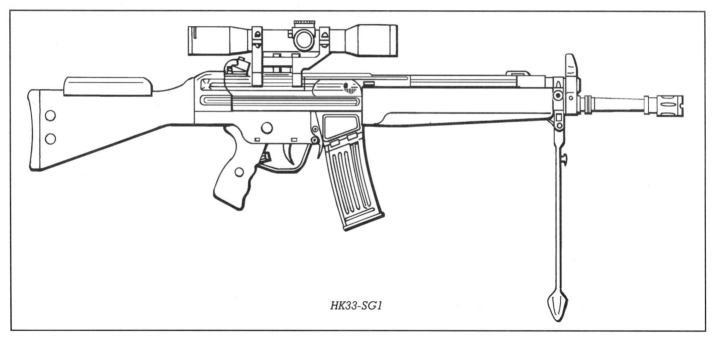

HK33-SG1

The Heckler & Koch HK33-SG 1 rifle with telescopic sight.

chamber, but it has to overcome the mechanical disadvantage of forcing two rollers out of engagement in recesses in the gun body before the movement can be transferred to the larger and heavier rear section of the bolt. It is this transfer which delays the opening of the bolt for long enough to permit the bullet to leave the muzzle and the chamber pressure to drop to a safe level before the case is extracted.

The **HK33-SG1** carries the normal iron sights but is also provided with a NATO-standard sight mount which will permit the fitting of any optical or electro-optical sight. The standard optical sight is a 4x telescope with range markers to 600 metres.

Other versions of the **HK33** include the standard fixed-butt rifle; standard rifle with telescoping butt; short-barrelled carbine; and rifle with bipod.

Data:

Chambering: 5.56 x 45mm NATO or M193
Operation: selective fire, delayed blowback
Length: 920mm (36.22in)
Weight: 3.65kg without sight (8.05 lbs)
Barrel: 390mm (15.35in), 6 grooves, right-hand twist, one turn in 178mm (7in) or 305mm (12in)
Magazine: 25-round box magazine
Muzzle velocity: 920 m/sec (3018 ft/sec)

Manufacturer:
Heckler & Koch UK, Nottingham, England

41

Heckler & Koch PSG-1

Germany

Whilst the 'stock' Heckler & Koch sniper rifles are perfectly satisfactory for median-range work, there are times when the sniper is called upon to deal with targets at long ranges, 800 or more metres away, and for this task a superior weapon is demanded. This is why the **PSG-1** (*Präzisions Scharfschützen Gewehr*) was designed.

Although the mechanism of the **PSG-1** is exactly the same as any other H&K rifle - a roller-locked delayed blowback system - the components are finished to a closer tolerance, and the remainder of the rifle is carefully built to suit. The barrel is 200mm longer than that of the standard rifle and is much heavier; it is rifled in Heckler & Koch's distinctive four-groove polygonal system which reduces friction on the bullet and, coupled with the additional barrel length, allows a higher velocity to be developed. The trigger is fully adjustable and has a pull-off of 1.5kg (3.3 lbs). The butt is also fully adjustable for length, rake, and height of cheek-piece, so that it can be fitted to any individual. There is a pistol grip, which itself is anatomically-shaped, and a precision tripod is also available.

No iron sights are fitted, a telescope sight mount to NATO-STANAG 2324 being built as an integral part of the rifle; this will accept any optical or electro-optical sight. The normal sight supplied is a 6x telescope with full adjustment for elevation and windage. An unusual refinement is a device for closing the bolt in silence, so that charging the weapon will not alert targets within earshot.

The usual 20-round magazine can be used, but a smaller 5-round magazine is

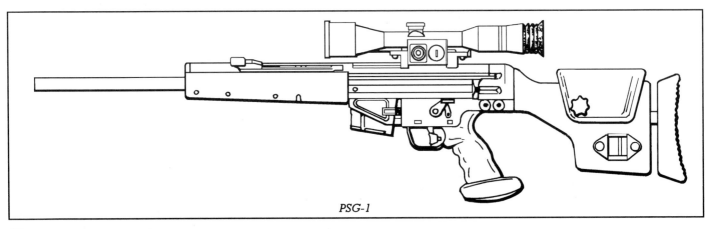

PSG-1

The Heckler & Koch PSG-1 mounted on its tripod.

also available, making the rifle more convenient for use in confined spaces. There is, of course, no provision for automatic fire in this weapon.

Using selected ammunition, test groups of under 80mm at 300 metres range are normal; although any service 7.62 x 51mm cartridge can be fired, the manufacturers recommend using match-grade commercial .308 Winchester ammunition for the most consistent results.

Manufacturer:
Heckler & Koch GmbH,
Oberndorf/Neckar, Germany

Data:

Chambering: 7.62 x 51mm NATO
Operation: roller-delayed blowback, semi-automatic
Length: 1208mm (47.55in)
Weight: 8.1 kg (17.86lbs) without sights or tripod
Barrel: 650mm (25.6in), 4 grooves, right-hand twist, polygonal.
Magazine: 5- or 20-round box
Muzzle velocity:
ca 900 m/sec (2952 ft/sec)

Heckler & Koch MSG-90   Germany

The **MSG-90** (Militär Scharfschützen Gewehr) is the most recent of Heckler & Koch sniping rifles and was designed to meet a military specification combining the robustness demanded of a field service weapon with the precision demanded for long range accurate shooting.

Whilst based upon the standard G3 rifle and using the same roller-locked delayed blowback operating system, the **MSG-90** is built to a generally more stringent set of tolerances. The barrel is heavier than standard, 150mm longer than standard, cold-forged, honed and tempered; the rifling is four-groove polygonal and is formed during the cold-forging operation. The stock is adjustable for length and height, the trigger unit is regulated to produce a consistent 1.5kg (3.3 lbs) pull, and there is an adjustable trigger shoe which enlarges the surface of the trigger to give more sensitive control. The fore-end is built with an internal T-rail which allows the fitting of an adjustable hand-stop or a shooting sling or bipod.

No iron sights are fitted. The receiver is formed with a NATO-STANAG 2324 sight mounting, so that virtually any optical or electro-optical sight can be attached. The normal sight provided by the makers is a 12 x telescope with range settings from 100 to 800 metres and full adjustment for elevation and windage.

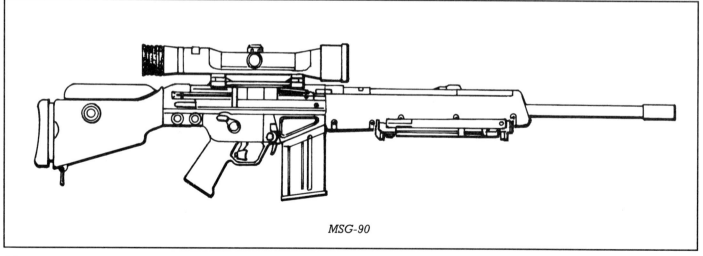

MSG-90

44

The Heckler & Koch MSG-90 sniping rifle with bipod folded.

The MSG-90 sniping rifle with bipod in use.

Data:

Chambering: 7.62 x 51mm NATO
Operation: roller-delayed blowback, semi-automatic
Length: 1165mm (45.87in)
Weight: 6.40kg (14.10lbs) without sights
Barrel: 600mm (23.62in),
four grooves, right-hand twist, polygonal
Magazine: 5- or 20-round box
Muzzle velocity:
ca 850 m/sec (2788 ft/sec)

Manufacturer:
Heckler & Koch GmbH,
Oberndorf/Neckar, Germany

Mauser SP66   Germany

The **SP66** is a heavy-barrelled bolt-action rifle which has been designed for the police and military. It uses the Gehmann bolt system, in which the front-lug bolt has its handle set just behind the bolt head and the magazine lies between the trigger and the bolt. This allows the bolt to be operated with much less disturbance than with a conventional design, which has the advantages of allowing a quicker return to the aim and also demanding less arm movement from the firer, so that there is less danger of him revealing his position.

The short bolt also allows the use of a lighter firing pin and stronger spring, so that the lock time - the time between pulling the trigger and the explosion of the cartridge - is in the order of 50 percent shorter than that of a conventional bolt.

The stock shows evidence of the influence of target rifles in the thumb-hole design and is fully adjustable for length and height. All surfaces which are to be handled are roughened and the fore-end is wide so as to offer the best possible grip for the supporting hand.

The heavy barrel is fitted with a combination flash hider and muzzle brake. The object here is not so much to conceal the firer's position than to prevent his being temporarily blinded by the flash, particularly when using optical sights. There are no iron sights on the rifle, but the receiver is fitted with a mount which accepts the standard optical sight, a Zeiss Diavari ZA zoom telescope giving 1.5x to 6x

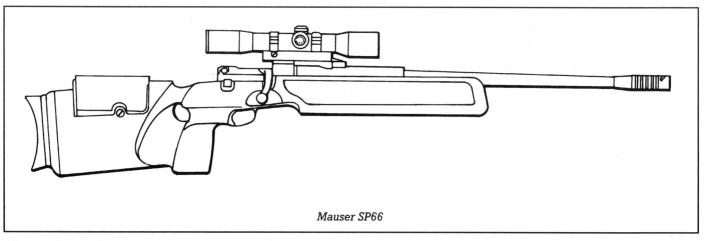

Mauser SP66

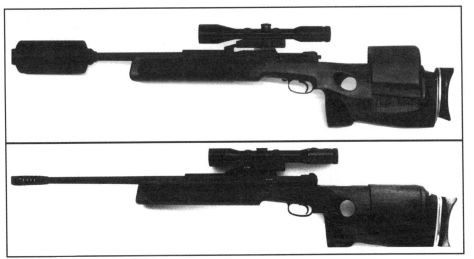

Data:

Chambering: 7.62 x 51mm NATO or .300 Winchester Magnum
Operation: Bolt action
Length: 1200mm (47.24in)
Weight: 6.12 kg (13.5lbs) with Zeiss telescope sight
Barrel: 650mm (25.6in), 4 grooves, right-hand twist, one turn in 305mm (12in).
Magazine: 3 rounds
Muzzle velocity: ca 860 m/sec (2820 ft/sec)

Manufacturer: Mauser-Werke Oberndorf GmbH, Germany

Top: The SP66 with silencer fitted. **Centre:** *The sniper rifle model SP66.* **Below:** *The Mauser SP66ilencer mode, dismantled for carriage.*

magnification. A second sight mount is provided, which adapts the rifle to NATO-STANAG 2324 and thus allows the use of most other optical and electro-optical sights.

The **SP66** is available chambered for the 7.62 x 51mm NATO cartridge or for the .300 Winchester Magnum cartridge, the latter being particularly favoured by police and security forces who are not, like most armies, tied to one particular cartridge by logistic demands.

The **Mauser 86** is offered as an alternative to the SP66 described previously. It returns to the more conventional type of bolt with two forward locking lugs and the handle at the rear. The heavy match grade, cold-forged barrel is fitted with a flash hider/muzzle brake and is bedded into the stock with artificial resin. The stock can be of laminated wood or of glass fibre in camouflage colours. In either case the butt is fully adjustable for length and height of cheek-piece and carries a recoil pad. There is a rail in the fore-end

to which a hand-stop, sling or bipod can be attached.

The barrel can be removed and a silenced barrel fitted in its place; the silencer is shorter and of larger diameter than most, but does not increase the overall length by very much and thus is easier to conceal than is usually the case.

Iron sights are not fitted as standard but can be supplied, the rear sight being micrometer-adjustable for elevation and windage, and the foresight being protected. Normally the rifle is used with a telescope sight, for which a dovetail

mount is provided on top of the receiver so that virtually any optical or electro-optical sight can be used. It is also possible to use the 'Teleranger' combination telescope sight and laser rangefinder

The trigger is adjustable and can be set either as a two-stage or single-stage release. Trigger slack, trigger pull and position of trigger are all adjustable externally, and the pull-off weight can be adjusted between 0.8 and 1.6 kg (28 and 56 oz).

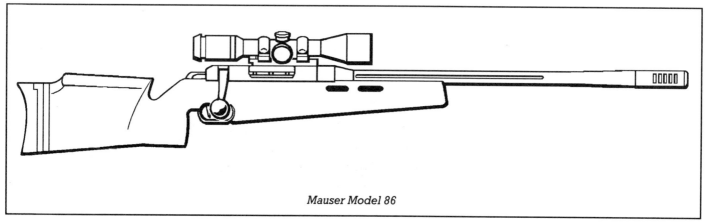

Mauser Model 86

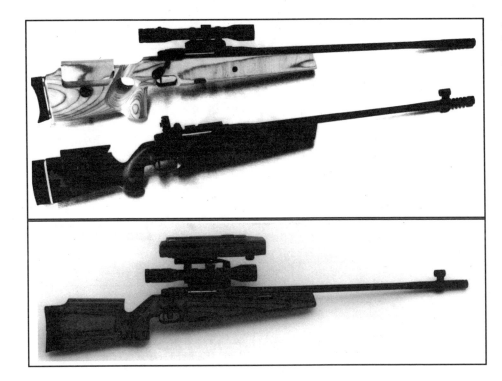

Left: *The Mauser Model 86 rifle with laminated wood and synthetic stocks.*

Below left: *The Mauser sniper rifle Model 86 with telescope and laser rangefinder.*

Data:

Chambering: 7.62 x 51mm NATO
Operation: Bolt action
Length: 1273mm (50.11in)
Weight: 6.20kg (13.66lbs)
Barrel: 650mm (25.6in), 4 grooves, right-hand twist, one turn in 305mm (12in).
Magazine: 9 rounds
Muzzle velocity: ca 860 m/sec (2820 ft/sec)

Manufacturer:
Mauser-WerkeOberndorf GmbH, Germany

Mauser SR93　　　　　　　　　　　　　Germany

Introduced in 1993, the **SR93** was developed in response to a German Army requirement for a sniping rifle capable of defeating body armour at 600 metres range. In order to achieve this, Mauser elected to chamber the rifle for either .300 Winchester Magnum or .338 Lapua Magnum cartridges but, recognising the expense of training snipers, have developed a change-over kit which adapts the rifle to fire 7.62 x 51mm NATO ammunition for training purposes.

The **SR93** is a conventional bolt action rifle, the bolt having two front locking lugs which provide a locking surface of $76mm^2$ $(1.18in^2)$ and a rotation of $90°$. The bolt is extremely unusual in that the handle can be removed and attached on the other side of the rifle to permit left-handed operation. This is also facilitated by duplicating the silent safety catch on both sides of the action.

The rifle is built up on a 'backbone' of cast magnesium-aluminium to which the various components are attached in the most ergonomic manner. The barrel is cold-forged and free-floating and is fitted with a muzzle brake. It is also deeply fluted so as to provide ample surfaces for the dissipation of heat. The skeleton butt is fully adjustable in all necessary directions, the cheek-piece being movable to either side. The fore-end and pistol grip are of synthetic material and the fore-end conceals a rail formed with the 'backbone' to which a bipod is fitted. This is infinitely adjustable and, like the remainder of the rifle, has no sharp edges or protuberances which could catch on clothing or undergrowth. The skeleton butt also conceals a monopod

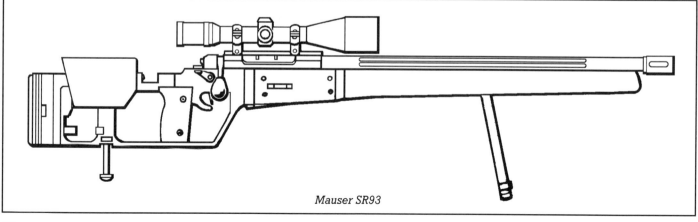

Mauser SR93

The Mauser Model SR93 with telescope and bipod.

leg which can be extended down so as to relieve the firer of weight while maintaining observation over a long period of time.

A sight mount is built on to the receiver, allowing any type of optical or electro-optical sight to be attached; Mauser make no stipulations over the sight but will supply whatever sight the user desires.

Using match grade ammunition, in either of the two calibres, the SR93 will put five shots at 100 metres range into a 25mm (one inch) circle.

Manufacturer:
Mauser-Werke Oberndorf GmbH, Germany

Data:
Chambering: .300 Winchester Magnum, .338 Lapua Magnum, (7.62 x 51mm NATO conversion available for training purposes)
Operation: Bolt action
Length: 1230mm (48.42in)
Weight: 5.90 kg (13.00lbs)
Barrel: 650mm (25.6in), 4 grooves, right-hand twist, one turn in 305mm (12in) standard, one turn in 254mm (10in) optional.
Magazine: 5 (.338) or 6 (.300) rounds
Muzzle velocity:
ca 915 m/sec (3000 ft/sec) with either cartridge, depending upon manufacturer.

51

Gepard M1   Hungary

It was to be expected that once the Western world began exploring the possibilities of the .50 Browning machine gun cartridge as a sniping round, the ex-Warsaw Pact countries would do the same for the Soviet 12.7 x 107mm cartridge, which is more or less their equivalent of the .50 Browning. The first of these to make an appearance was the **M1 Gepard** from Hungary.

The **Gepard** is a single-shot rifle with an unusual breech action. The pistol grip is part of a self-contained unit which has,

at the front, a multiple-lug breechblock, and at the rear a hammer and striker system. To operate, the pistol grip is rotated upwards to the right so as to unlock the breech, drawn back and removed completely. The cartridge can then be inserted into the breech. The breech block unit is then replaced, the pistol grip being turned down to lock, and the hammer is then manually cocked. The firer then takes aim and pulls the trigger.

There is a substantial recoil force from

the 12.7mm cartridge and the body of the rifle is therefore carried in a sleeve-like cradle within which it can recoil, damped by springs. This, together with the large muzzle brake, reduces the felt recoil to something in the order of a large-calibre hunting rifle. The butt is provided with a cushioned cheek-rest, and the rear monopod leg carries a useful grip for the firer's disengaged hand. The weight of the rifle is taken by a bipod attached to the front of the cradle.

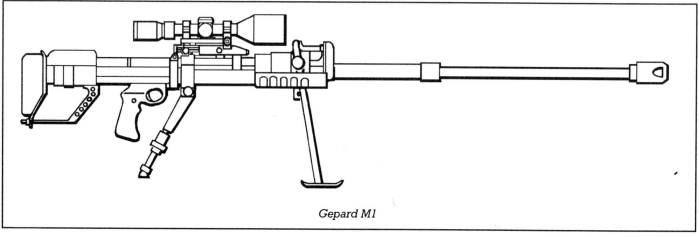

Gepard M1

The accuracy of the 12.7mm bullet is comparable with that of the .50 Browning and can be expected to put a five-round group into a 300mm (11.8in) circle at 600 metres range. The penetrative power is such that the AP bullet can penetrate 15mm (0.6in) of steel armour at the same range. The manufacturers claim a maximum effective range of 2000 metres against a vehicle-sized target.

Rudimentary iron sights are fitted, for emergency use only; the normal sight is a 12x telescope sight fitted to a permanent mount above the cradle. Since cradle and barrel are separate items and move independently of each other, the maintenance of zero in this weapon could require some vigilance.

There is a variant model of the **Gepard**, known as the M1A1; this is the same weapon but is mounted on a back-pack frame which also acts as the ground mount.

Top: *The Hungarian Gepard M1 heavy sniping rifle.*

Above: *The Gepard M1A1 rifle on its sled mounting, with bipod folded.*

Data:

Chambering: 12.7 x 107mm Soviet
Operation: Bolt action
Length: 1570mm (61.8in)
Weight: 19 kg (41.88 lbs)
Barrel: 1100mm (43.3in)
Magazine: None; single shot
Muzzle velocity:
840 m/sec (2756 ft/sec)

Manufacturer:
Technika, Budapest. Hungary

Gepard M2   Hungary

This followed the Gepard M1 and differed in being a semi-automatic weapon; the makers saw this as more an anti-materiel weapon than as an anti-personnel weapon and thus felt the need for more rapid fire than the peculiar breech action of the M1 could manage.

Like the M1, the **M2** has the barrel and action supported in a tubular cradle which also contains springs to absorb some of the recoil force. At the same time these springs also assist in the semi-automatic operation, which is on the principle of long recoil. The ammunition is carried in a magazine which lies alongside the pistol grip. After fitting the loaded magazine, the bolt is pulled back and released, which collects a cartridge from the magazine and loads it. On firing, the entire action, barrel and bolt together, recoils backwards for about five inches and then stops. The bolt is unlocked during the last inch or so of this movement, and is then held firmly. The barrel, under the influence of its springs, now runs forward and into the firing position. During this movement the barrel is pulled off the empty cartridge case, and, as soon as the case is free of the chamber, a mechanical ejector knocks it out of the feedway. Once the barrel has stopped moving, the bolt is released, to run forward, collect a new cartridge and chamber it, and then lock into the barrel once more, leaving the firing hammer cocked and the rifle ready for the next shot.

As might be imagined, all this movement absorbs quite a large amount of the recoil force and the **M2** is therefore much more pleasant to fire than is the M1.

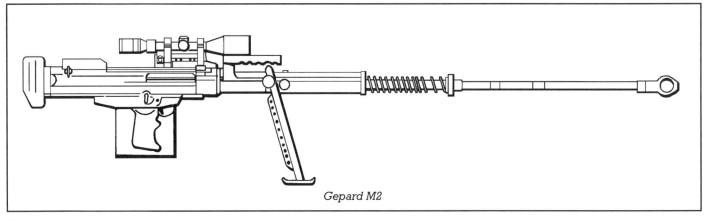

Gepard M2

In other respects the rifle is much the same as the M1, uses the same type of sight and fires the same ammunition, though the makers claim a maximum effective range of only 1000 metres for the M2.

There is also an **M2A1** variant model, intended for use by airborne and other special forces requiring a shorter weapon. It is simply the M2 design but with a shorter barrel and a somewhat larger muzzle brake in order to dissipate the extra muzzle blast usefully.

Top: *The Hungarian Gepard M2 rifle; note that the magazine lies alongside the pistol grip.*

Above: *The Gepard M2A1 is a shorter and lighter version of the M2.*

Data

Chambering: 12.7 x 107mm Soviet
Operation: Semi-automatic, long recoil
Length: 1530mm °(60.23in)
Weight: 12.0 kg (26.45lbs)
Barrel: 1100mm (43.3in)
Magazine: 5 or 10 rounds, side-mounted
Muzzle velocity: 840 m/sec (2756 ft/sec)

Manufacturer:
Technika, Budapest. Hungary

Gepard M3 — Hungary

The third member of the Gepard family is, as might be expected, the M2 model upgraded to fire the 14.5 x 115mm Soviet cartridge.

It is worth recalling that although now associated with the KPV heavy machine gun, the 14.5mm round was actually developed for use in two Soviet anti-tank rifles, the PTRD and PTRS, during World War Two. It gave them a formidable performance, so much so that the Soviets retained them in use until the war ended, whereas almost every other user of anti-tank rifles had discarded them by 1943.

(It is also a commentary on the changing times to note that neither of these wartime rifles had very much in the way of recoil-absorbing devices.)

The **Gepard M3** (which was originally called the 'Destroyer') is simply an enlarged and strengthened version of the M2. It uses the same long recoil system of operation in which the entire action and barrel recoil back in the receiver for a distance rather longer than a complete cartridge. The bolt is then held fast while the barrel runs back into battery, stripping itself away from the

spent cartridge case as it does so. The cartridge case now has to be mechanically ejected, after which the bolt is released to run forward, chamber a fresh cartridge and lock. In order to absorb the recoil there is an hydraulic buffer inside the cradle, together with a spring recuperator to return the mechanism to the firing position after the recoil has been soaked up. There is also a muzzle brake of generous proportions to trap most of the muzzle blast and direct it sideways so as to assist in reducing the recoil force.

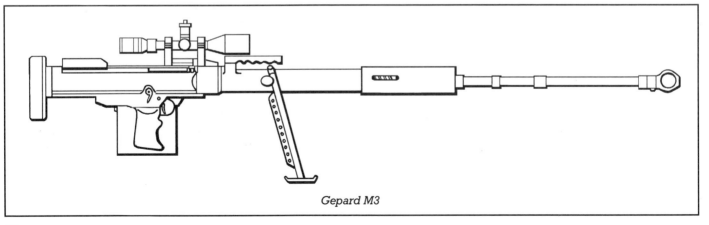

Gepard M3

The 14.5mm cartridge fires a 64 gram (988 grain) bullet at about 1000 m/sec to develop about 32,000 Joules (23,600 foot-pounds) of energy at the muzzle. With this sort of power the armour-piercing bullet can penetrate 25mm (one inch) of armour plate at 600 metres range, and even the ball bullet can do immense damage to equipment.

Data:

Chambering: 14.5 x 114mm Soviet
Operation: Semi-automatic, long recoil
Length: 1880mm (74.0in)
Weight: 20.0 kg (44.1 lbs)
Barrel: 1480mm (58.27in)
Magazine: 5 or 10 rounds, side-mounted
Muzzle velocity: ca 1000 m/sec (3280 ft/sec)

Manufacturer:
Technika, Budapest. Hungary

Above: Breech, pistol grip and magazine of the Gepard M3 rifle.

Below: The Gepard M3 heavy sniping rifle.

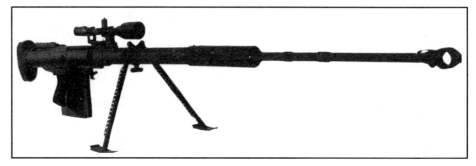

Galil Sniper   Israel

The Galil rifle is the standard rifle of the Israeli Defence Force, adopted in the early 1970s. It owes a good deal to the Kalashnikov design and has proved itself to be a reliable and serviceable combat weapon.

Soon after its introduction the Israel Defence Force expressed a desire for a sniping rifle and Major Israel Galil, designer of the rifle, working in close co-operation with the Defence Force, developed this sniping version which was announced in 1982. The requirement was that the rifle should put all its shots into a 12 to 15cm (4 to 6 inches) circle at 300 metres range and a 30cm (11.8in) circle at 600 metres range with standard ammunition, and this the **Galil Sniper** will certainly do. And with selected grade match ammunition it will usually do rather better.

The mechanism is that of the standard rifle, a gas-operated weapon using a rotating bolt inside a bolt carrier which is propelled by the gas piston. The mechanism is arranged for semi-automatic fire only, the selective-fire facility of the standard Galil rifle having no application in the sniping role. There are, though, several features unique to the sniping weapon. There is a strong bipod attached to the front end of the receiver so that no stress is placed on the barrel, which is heavier than standard. The mount for the telescope sight is a precision casting and fits on to the left side of the receiver. It is a long-base unit and gives very steady support to the standard 6 x 40 telescope sight.

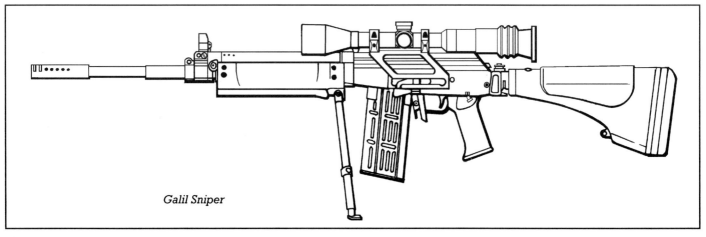

Galil Sniper

The 7.62mm Galil sniper rifle ready for use.

Data:

Chambering: 7.62 x 51mm NATO
Operation: Semi-automatic, gas, rotating bolt
Length: 1115m (43.9in) butt extended; 840mm (33.1in) butt folded
Weight: 6.40 kg with bipod (14.1 lbs)
Barrel: 508mm (20 in), 4 grooves, right-hand twist, one turn in 305mm (12in).
Magazine: 20 rounds
Muzzle velocity: 815 m/sec (2674 ft/sec)

Manufacturer:
Israel Military Industries, Ramat Ha'Sharon,. Israel

The mount is designed so that it can be quickly removed from the rifle for transport and replaced without requiring the weapon to be re-zeroed. A night sight can be fitted in place of the standard telescope if required.

The barrel is fitted with a combined muzzle brake and compensator which reduces the recoil force and also damps out any tendency for the muzzle to rise on firing, thus allowing rapid realignment of the sights after each shot. The muzzle brake can be removed and a silencer attached in its place; it is recommended that the silencer only be used with sub-sonic ammunition.

The trigger is a two-stage military type with adjustment for pull-off pressure. The butt-stock can be folded, to make the rifle more compact for transport. When unfolded it locks perfectly rigid, and the shoulder-pad and cheek-rest are both adjustable.

The rifle is supplied in a special transit case which also carries the telescope sight and mount, optical filters for the telescope, a carrying and firing sling, two magazines, and a cleaning outfit.

The Galil sniper rifle with butt and bipod folded for carriage.

59

Beretta Sniper   Italy

The Beretta company have been in the firearms business since the 16th century and have produced a wide variety of military and sporting weapons. In 1984 they introduced a new line of sporting rifles, the 500 Series, based on a Mauser-type bolt action and chambered for a range of hunting cartridges. In order to accommodate chamberings from .22 Remington to .375 Holland & Holland Magnum, the bolt action and receiver were produced in three sizes, and the degree of finish was more or less proportional to what the customer was prepared to pay.

At this time the Italian Army was contemplating a sniping rifle, and it approached Beretta. Beretta responded with a special version of the 500 Series using the medium-length bolt action and receiver attached to a specially-developed heavy barrel. This had a conical flash-hider on the muzzle and was carefully rifled and lapped to tight tolerances.

The stock was specially designed, based upon target-shooting practice, and uses a thumb-hole buttstock and a wide 'beavertail' fore-end which conceals a mounting rail and a tube containing an harmonic balancer. This is a spring-and-weight device which absorbs and damps the barrel vibration which occurs when a shot is fired and this, if not controlled, can frequently ruin any chance of accuracy irrespective of how well the barrel has been made. The front end of the balancer tube mounts a bipod.

The buttstock is fitted with an adjustable cheek-piece and recoil pad; a hand-stop can be fitted on to the mounting rail in the fore-end, and a firing sling can also be fitted to the rail.

Target-quality iron sights are fitted; the foresight is hooded to reduce reflection and glare, and the rear sight is micrometer-adjustable for windage and

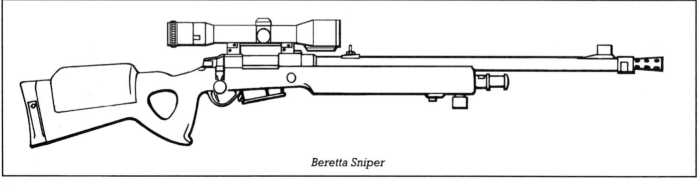

Beretta Sniper

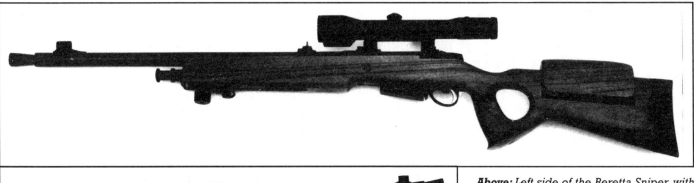

Above: Left side of the Beretta Sniper, with bipod folded.

Left: The 7.62mm Beretta Sniper in firing position.

elevation. However, as with all sniping rifles, a telescope is the normal method of sighting and unless otherwise specified, the **Beretta Sniper** comes with a Zeiss 1.6 to 6x zoom telescope sight. The sight mount is to NATO-STANAG 2324 so that any military-pattern optical or electro-optical sight can be fitted.

Data:

Chambering: 7.62 x 51mm NATO
Operation: Bolt action
Length: 1165mm (45.87in)
Weight: 5.55kg (12.24lbs)
Barrel: 586mm (23.07in), 4 grooves, right-hand twist,
one turn in 305mm (12in).
Magazine: 5 rounds
Muzzle velocity: 845 m/sec (2772 ft/sec)

Manufacturer:
Armi Beretta, Gardone Val Trompia, Italy

This is probably the last Mauser 1898-action rifle to survive in military service, which says a lot for the fundamental soundness of the Mauser 98 action. It was developed by Vapensmia, a small gunmaking firm, in cooperation with Norwegian military and police experts. One of the criteria for any sniping rifle (or any other firearm) in Scandinavia is that it must work infallibly in extreme cold conditions, and for this reason semi-automatic sniping rifles are not generally welcome. A semi-automatic general service rifle is acceptable, since it will be continually handled, frequently fired and thus usually warm enough to function well; and if it stutters a little on the first couple of rounds, that will be all. But a sniping rifle cannot afford to fail and is liable to be lying in the cold for hours before being called upon to fire. For this reason, bolt actions, and well-tried bolt actions at that, are the preferred weapons. And even they have to be carefully designed to prevent freezing up.

The **NM149S** resembles a sporting rifle, except that it is a good deal more robust than most commercial rifles. The heavy barrel is carefully bedded into a stock made from impregnated and laminated beechwood. The butt is adjustable for length by inserting spacers between the butt and the shoulder pad; the police model is provided with an adjustable cheekpiece, but the military version does not have one. The match trigger is adjusted for a 1.5kg pull and has a very distinct and crisp release.

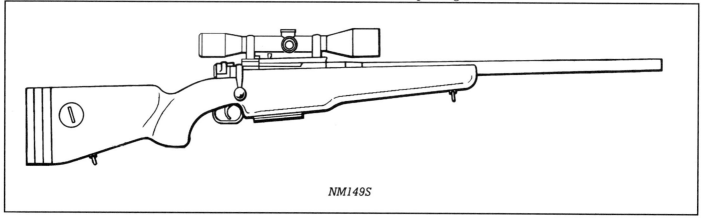

NM149S

Iron sights are provided for emergency use, but the normal sight is a Schmidt & Bender 6 x 42 telescope fitted into a mount which allows it to be removed and replaced without affecting the zero of the rifle. It is also prepared for fitting a Simrad KN250 night vision sight unit which (as is described on another page) will permit the ordinary telescope to be used at night and thus does away with the problem of re-zeroing the rifle for a night sight.

The fore-end is prepared for the attachment of a bipod if required, and the muzzle for the attachment of a silencer, both being offered as optional equipment.

Above: The Norwegian NM149S sniping rifle.
Left: The Norwegian NM149S with Simrad KN250 night vision sight attached to the normal telescope sight.

Data:

Chambering: 7.62 x 51mm NATO
Operation: Bolt action
Length: 1120mm (44.1in)
Weight: 5.60kg (12.34lbs) with telescope
Barrel: 600mm (23.6in), 4 grooves, right-hand twist, one turn in 305mm (12in).
Magazine: 5 rounds
Muzzle velocity: 838 m/sec (2750 ft/sec)

Manufacturer:
Vapensmia A/S, Dokka, Norway

VSS Silent Sniper   Russia

This is a weapon which is virtually unknown outside Russia and thus all the data comes from the promoters and must be taken at its face value.

The **VSS** mechanism is based upon that of the Kalashnikov rifle, using a similar gas-actuated rotating bolt and carrier system, and is the same as that used in the MA submachine gun. This is allied to an integral barrel/silencer unit which it is claimed to combine an exceptionally low noise level with greater range, accuracy and penetrating power than is generally expected of silenced weapons. According to the brochures the silencer is on the dual chamber principle, in which the propelling gas is allowed to bleed from holes in the rifle's barrel and into a primary chamber. There the gases expand and then pass via a series of mesh filters into a second chamber which further reduces the pressure before releasing the gases to the atmosphere. There appears to be little that is novel in this arrangement.

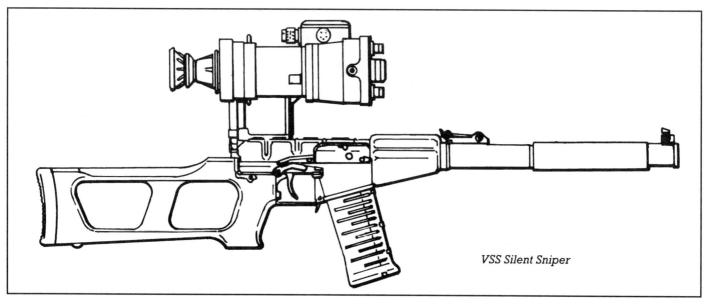

VSS Silent Sniper

The rifle has a short fore-end, a pistol grip, and a stock which folds sideways to lie alongside the receiver. A sight mount on the left side of the receiver will accept any standard Russian sight unit, optical or electro-optical, but, of course, will not accept any Western sight.

The heart of the system is the special ammunition. The 9 x 39mm SP-5 round is based upon the standard Russian M1943 39mm case with the mouth opened up to take a 16.3 gram 9mm bullet. The bullet contains a tungsten or hardened steel core/tip and, it is claimed, will penetrate 6mm of armour at 100 metres and 2mm at 500 metres range. The round is also said to be sub-sonic; this means a muzzle velocity in the order of 330 m/sec, and it is difficult to understand how a 16.3g bullet launched at that speed can retain sufficient energy to defeat armour at 500 metres range. It is also apparent that the trajectory at 500 metres - or even half that distance - will be far from flat, and precision shooting therefore becomes something of a gamble. This may be a 'sniping' weapon at short range, but it seems to be far from the generally accepted picture of sniping.

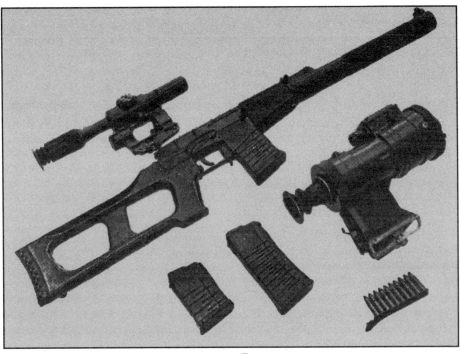

The Russian VSS and its many accessories.

Manufacturer:
Institute of Precise Mechanical Engineering, Izhevsk, Russia

Data:

Chambering: 9 x 39mm Soviet
Operation: Selective fire, gas
Length: 894mm (35.2in)
Weight: 2.60kg (5.73lbs)
Barrel: Not known
Magazine: 10 or 20 rounds
Muzzle velocity:
Less than 330 m/sec (1080 ft/sec).

Dragunov SVD

Russia

By comparison with the myriad of wonder weapons which have been announced from Russia since 1990, the **Dragunov** sniping rifle is a conventional, no-nonsense weapon which has acquired a sound reputation for reliability and accuracy based upon actual tested performance.

It entered Soviet service in the latter 1960s and soon spread to other Communist bloc countries, as well as being manufactured under licence in China, Romania and Iran.

The **Dragunov**, like most current Russian weapons, is broadly based upon the mechanism of the Kalashnikov rifle but with an important difference. It is chambered for the 7.62x54R cartridge, a powerful round dating from the 1890s

and, like most rifle rounds of that era, effective to well beyond 1000 metres range. It is also a rimmed cartridge, and the combination of shape and power mean that the 'pure' Kalashnikov system of gas piston and rotating bolt is not suitable. The bolt has to be redesigned to deal with the larger rimmed cartridge case, and, more importantly, the operating cycle has to be changed from the 'long stroke' gas piston of the Kalashnikov to a 'short stroke' system better suited to the pressure characteristics of the older cartridge. Instead of driving a piston which is directly connected to the bolt carrier, the piston in the **Dragunov** rifle makes a short and fast stroke to strike the head of an operating rod, and it is the

momentum of this operating rod which then carries out the extracting and reloading cycle. A further advantage of this system is that the moving mass is considerably lighter and, therefore, the disturbance of the rifle, due to the oscillation of the bolt carrier and piston, is much less, allowing a quicker return to a precise aim.

The rifle can be fitted with any Russian optical or optronic sight and is generally found with the PSO-1, a 4 x 24 telescope; iron sights are fitted for use in an emergency. There is no provision for automatic fire, but, unusually for a sniping rifle, there is a bayonet lug on the muzzle allowing the fitting of the standard service bayonet.

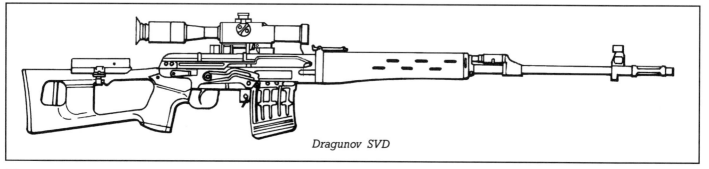

Dragunov SVD

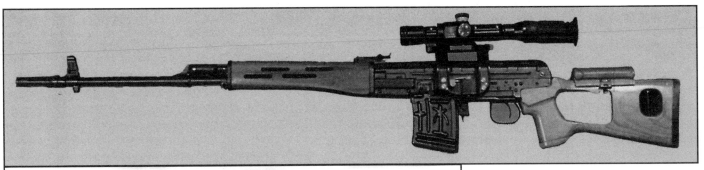

Above: *The Russian 7.62mm Dragunov sniping rifle.*

Left: *Close-up of the Dragunov reciever and sight.*

Manufacturer:
Izhevsk Rifle Factory, Izhevsk, Russia

Data:

Chambering: 7.62x54R Soviet
Operation: Semi-automatic, gas
Length: 1225mm (48.23in) Weight:
4.30kg (9.48lbs) with PSO-1 sight
Barrel: 622mm (24.48in), 4 grooves,
right-hand twist,
one turn in 254mm (10in)
Magazine: 10 rounds
Muzzle Velocity: 830 m/sec (2723ft/sec)

Aerotek are a small South African firm which cut their teeth on a 12.7mm sniping rifle, then set about producing a 14.5mm weapon to fire the big Russian cartridge which is fairly common in the African continent, and have finally gone for the ultimate in building a rifle around a 20mm cannon cartridge. In fact their big rifle is virtually the same in both large calibres, only the barrel, bolt, magazine and sights require changing in order to adapt the rifle to fire either 14.5mm or 20mm ammunition.

In either calibre the **NTW** rifle is a single-shot, bolt action repeater capable of being fired from the shoulder. The barrel and action slide inside a body which carries the butt, pistol grip and bipod, and the two units are connected by the 'Aerotek Recoil Management System' which could be described as an artillery gun recoil system suitably scaled down. On firing, the barrel and action slide back in the body unit, the movement damped and controlled by the recoil system, after which they are returned to the firing position and

the firer can operate the bolt to reload. The effect upon the firer is said to be roughly the same as a magnum-calibre hunting rifle. The box magazine fits into the left side of the gun body.

To facilitate movement, the barrel can be quickly removed, so that one man can carry the barrel, sights and magazines, while the other carries the gun body and receiver. Special manpacks have been developed to simplify carrying the two sections.

In 14.5mm calibre the rifle has an operational range from 300 to

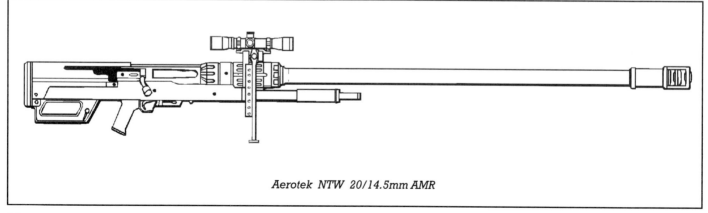

Aerotek NTW 20/14.5mm AMR

2300 metres (330 to 2515yards) and a very good armour-piercing capability. In 20mm calibre the range is 150 to 1500 metres (165 to 1650 yards); the AP capability is less, but in this calibre the firer has a wide choice of explosive and incendiary projectiles capable of doing a great deal more damage than a simple ball bullet.

The sight, for both rifles, is an 8 x 42 telescope with parallax correction, fitted to a mount which incorporates a range drum calibrated to the particular ammunition.

The Aerotek NTW rifle in two units for carriage.

Top: *The 20mm version of the Aerotek rifle; note the shorter and smooth barrel.*

Data: for 14.5mm;
(for 20mm where different)
Chambering: 14.5 x 114mm
(20 x 82mm)
Operation: Bolt action repeater
Length: 2015mm (79.3in)
1795mm (70.7in)
Weight: 28kg (61.7lbs)
26kg (57.3lbs)
Barrel: Not known
Magazine: 3-round box
Muzzle velocity:
1080 m/sec (3540ft/sec)
720 m/sec (2360 ft/sec)

Manufacturer:
Aerotek, Pretoria, South Africa

M76 Serbia

This rifle is of considerable interest, particularly when compared with the Russian Dragunov (q.v.) because it lies at the opposite pole of opinion. The Dragunov, as explained in that entry, has gone to a great deal of trouble to change the gas actuating system from a long stroke piston to a short stroke impulse system in order to avoid shifts of balance and to better suit the ballistics of an old-fashioned high-powered, full-size cartridge. The **M76** uses one of the oldest and most powerful of military rifle cartridges, the Mauser 7.92 x 57mm

round, but does it with a 'pure' Kalashnikov long-stroke piston system.

The **M76** was developed in the late 1970s as a member of a new series of rifles and machine guns based upon the Kalashnikov design but chambered for Western cartridges, the object being export sales. Beyond equipping some parts of the Yugoslavian armed forces, however, it seems unlikely that much export trade took place before Yugoslavia disintegrated.

At bottom, the **M76** is a Kalashnikov with a longer and heavier barrel than

usual, and this, together with the use of better cartridges, is the reason for its improved accuracy and adoption as a sniping weapon. The barrel is 550mm long, in contrast to the 415mm of the normal AK-type rifle, and, of course, the 7.92mm cartridge is ballistically superior to the 7.62 x 39mm round. The makers claimed that the effective range was 800 metres, and we see no reason to dispute that.

The gas piston system is pure Kalashnikov; the gas is tapped off a little farther ahead of the chamber, but drives

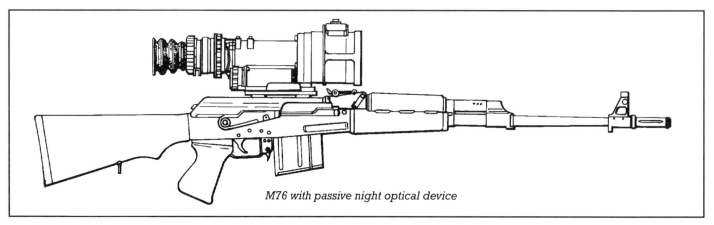

M76 with passive night optical device

the same type of piston, which is formed into a bolt carrier at its rear end and carries the rotating bolt. The longer barrel allows the propelling gases to expand after the all-burnt point and this leads to a better consistency in velocity and hence a better accuracy. Doubtless the different pressure curve of the Mauser cartridge suits the piston system better than that of the Russian 7.62 x 54R cartridge and this, together with a somewhat more practical view of the sniper's task, has led the Yugoslavian designer to ignore the Dragunov's short-stroke system. After all, most snipers do what is wanted with one shot and are not particularly excited about going to extremes of mechanical design in order to allow them to return to the aim one second quicker.

The usual iron sights are fitted, but the receiver has a mount which accepts a Yugoslavian sight (designation unknown) which appears to have been copied from the Soviet PSO-1 used with the Dragunov rifle. It is of the same 4 x 24 power and is of the same size and appearance as the PSO-1.

Top: The M76 semi-automatic sniper rifle with passive night optical device.

Above: The Serbian M76 sniping rifle is simply a lengthened Kalashnikov.

Manufacturer:
Zastava Arms, Belgrade, Serbia

Data:

Chambering: 7.92 x 57mm Mauser; other options available
Operation: Semi-automatic, gas
Length: 1135mm (44.68in)
Weight: 4.20 kg (9.26lbs)
Barrel: 550mm (21.65in) , 4 grooves, right-hand twist, one turn in 240mm (9.45in)
Magazine: 10 rounds
Muzzle velocity: 720 m/sec (2362 ft/sec)

SIG have been making rifles for the Swiss Army since 1864, some of which were adapted for sniping, but it was not until the 1970s that they began manufacture of specialised military sniping rifles, using their accumulated knowledge of sporting and target rifles.

The **SSG2000** is a bolt action rifle using a unique system developed by J.P. Sauer of Germany and used on the Sauer 80/90 series of sporting rifles. It differs from the usual type of bolt in not having lugs on the bolt head, but instead it has four lugs towards the rear of the bolt. These take the form of wedges which lie inside the bolt body and are forced out by cam action as the bolt handle is turned down when the bolt is closed. The bolt body does not revolve, merely the handle, and, as it turns, so the four lugs are pressed out to wedge into recesses in the receiver body. This also produces a bolt with a turning angle of only 65°, calling for less movement on the part of the firer and not causing any interference with the sight mounting.

The heavy barrel is cold-hammered and fitted with a combination muzzle brake, flash hider and compensator, which helps to conceal the discharge, absorbs some of the recoil force and helps to prevent excessive muzzle rise on firing.

The thumb-hole stock is fully adjustable to suit the firer, and for left-handed firers a left-handed stock can be provided.

The trigger is a double set type, and a sliding safety catch locks the sear, sear pivot and bolt, though the bolt can be opened when the safety is applied. The set trigger can be de-cocked by pulling the trigger when the safety catch is in the safe position, and also by opening the bolt. There is also a signal pin which indicates when a round is in the chamber.

No iron sights are provided, but the receiver is shaped to accept most types of optical sight. The recommended patterns are the Zeiss Diatal ZA 8 x 50 or the Schmidt & Bender 1.5-6 x 42 zoom sight. The **SSG2000** has been widely adopted by police and security forces all over the world.

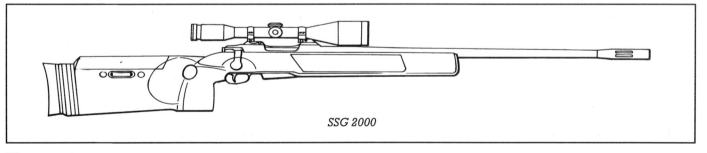

SSG 2000

The SIG SSG2000 sniping rifle on its tripod.

Manufacturer
SIG, Neuhausen, Switzerland

Data:

Chambering: 7.62 x 51mm NATO;
other options available
Operation: Bolt action
Length: 1210mm (47.64in)
Weight: 6.60 kg (14.55 lbs) with sight
Barrel: 610mm(24.01in),4 grooves,
right-hand twist,
one turn in 305mm (12in).
Magazine: 4 rounds
Muzzle velocity:
ca 800 m/sec (2625 ft/sec)

SIG SSG 3000

Because of the stringent Swiss regulations on the export of firearms, SIG established a working relationship with the German J.P. Sauer company several years ago, the best-known result of which are the SIG-Sauer pistols, designed by SIG and made by Sauer for worldwide export. The relationship also works the other way, and this rifle is based upon the Sauer 200 STR target rifle, using a more conventional front-lug bolt having two banks of three lugs on a reduced-diameter head, locking into the barrel.

The rifle is built on a modular system. The barrel is joined to the receiver by a screw clamp and the trigger unit is a separately removable assembly. Two trigger systems are available, a single-stage trigger or a double-stage trigger, both being fully adjustable for length of pull and take-up weight. The sliding safety catch locks the trigger, firing pin and bolt, and there is a visual and tactile indicator pin which shows whether or not the chamber is loaded.

The stock has been carefully designed to permit full adjustment for height,

length, offset and rake, and for left-handed shooters there is a completely left-handed version of the rifle available. The stock is made of a non-warping wood laminate, and the fore-end encloses a rail to which a hand-stop, sling or bipod can be attached.

The cold-hammered heavy barrel carries a similar flash hider, muzzle brake and compensator to that used on the SSG2000 rifle. There are no iron sights, the top of the receiver being shaped for a telescope mount. The standard mount is designed to suit the recommended telescope sight, the Hensoldt 1.5-6 x 24 BL, which has been designed and built specifically for this rifle. However, the receiver can also be supplied with a NATO-STANAG 2324 sight base to permit the fitting of a wide variety of optical and electro-optical sights if required.

An unusual accessory for this rifle is a .22 rimfire conversion kit which permits the use of cheap .22 Long Rifle ammunition for training and practice purposes.

The SIG SSG 3000 rifle, showing the anti-glare screen stretched over the barrel, the flash suppressor/muzzle brake and the adjustable bipod.

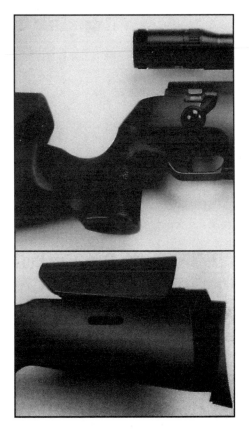

Above left: The well-designed pistol grip.

Left: The wide range of adjustment of the cheek piece and butt pad enable them to be fitted to any firer.

Above : The most recent version of the SSG 3000 shows a slight change in the design of the muzzle brake.

Manufacturer:
SIG, Neuhausen, Switzerland

Data:

Chambering: 7.62 x 51mm NATO and other options
Operation: Bolt action
Length: 1180mm (46.45in)
Weight: 5.40 kg (11.90 lbs)
Barrel:
610mm (24.01in), 4 grooves, right-hand twist, one turn in 305mm (12in).
Magazine: 5 rounds
Muzzle velocity:
ca 800 m/sec (2625 ft/sec)

SIG SG550   Switzerland

The **SG 550** is the standard service rifle of the Swiss Army under the title 'Sturmgewehr 90'. It is in 5.56mm calibre and it therefore made sense for the Swiss Army to request a sniping rifle using the same cartridge and based upon their standard rifle, so saving time in training and simplifying their ammunition supply. The **SG550** was the solution offered by SIG and it is now in use by the Swiss police, SwissArmy and others. The basic **SG 550** is a gas-operated selective-fire rifle using the usual sort of rotating bolt to close and lock the breech, and this system is retained but modified so that only semi-automatic action is available. The barrel, however, is heavier and longer than the standard rifle and no iron sights are fitted. The stock is considerably different, allowing adjustment for length and for height of cheek-rest, and it is also capable of being folded sideways to lie alongside the receiver for storage or transport.

The pistol-grip has an adjustable hand rest, and there is a fully adjustable bipod which can be attached to the fore-end.

As with other SIG precision rifles there is a screen which can be stretched across the top of the rifle so as to divert the hot air rising from the barrel so that it does not disturb the line of sight; it also prevents reflections from the metalwork interfering with the firer's sight picture or revealing his position.

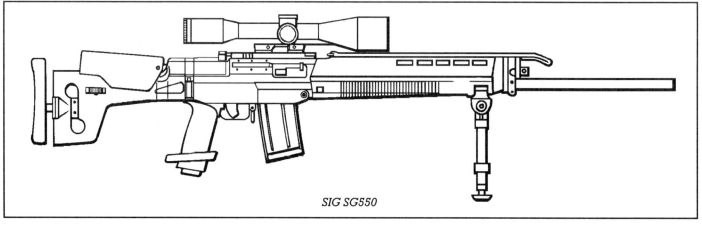

SIG SG550

The receiver is formed to take a sighting telescope; SIG make no particular recommendations as to the type used, and no doubt this mount can be provided in various styles to suit the user's requirements.

All this adds up to a very sound precision rifle. The heavy barrel, bipod and adjustable stock, when allied to the 5.56mm cartridge, mean low recoil forces and little or no disturbance of the aim, and the semi-automatic action means that a second shot can be got off much more rapidly than with most other sniping rifles.

Data:

Chambering: 5.56 x 45mm NATO
Operation: Semi-automatic, gas
Length:
1130mm (44.48in) butt extended;
905mm (35.63in) butt folded
Weight: 7.02 kg (15.48 lbs)
Barrel: 650mm (25.6in), 6 grooves,
right-hand twist,
one turn in 254mm (10in).
Magazine: 20 or 30 rounds
Muzzle velocity:
ca 1000 m/sec. (3280 ft/sec)

Manufacturer:
SIG, Neuhausen, Switzerland

Top left: *The SIG SG550 sniper rifle with day telescope sight. Note the translucent plastic magazine*
Top right: *The SIG SG550SP is the commercially available version of the SG550; note the triple magazine assembly, allowing a very fast change of magazines. This is standard on all Swiss service rifles.*
Above: *The SIG SG550 sniper rifle with night vision sight.*

Armalon Model BGR

The **Armalon BGR** is a carefully designed and built conventional bolt-action rifle of high quality. The company has been producing this rifle for several years, building it up from components supplied by a number of specialist manufacturers and fine-tuning the design in response to the requirements of the customers.

The bolt action is a strengthened bench-rest action based on Mauser lines and using a three-lug lockup and a long and smooth bolt movement. The firing pin has been carefully designed to provide the shortest possible lock time and also to deliver a blow which will ensure ignition with even the hardest caps. The heavy barrel is hammer-forged and rifled and lapped to match standards. It is also fluted so as to present the maximum cooling area and also to achieve the maximum stiffness without excess weight. A muzzle brake and compensator on the muzzle reduce the felt recoil and also counter the tendency of the muzzle to lift on firing.

The stock may be of wood, or of carbon fibre-based synthetic material; or, for the utmost lightness combined with strength, a specially formulated composition of carbon fibre, Kevlar and glass-reinforced plastic has been developed. In whatever stock is chosen, the barrel is bedded-in by means of a specially prepared compound.

The fore-end carries an Anschütz-type rail which will accept a hand stop, sling or bipod. Iron sights are not normally fitted, though they can be provided if

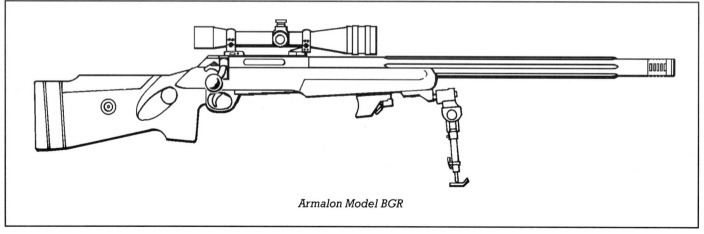

Armalon Model BGR

The 7.62mm Armalon BGR sniping rifle with sling and ammunition.

required; the receiver is prepared for mounting a variety of optical or electro-optical sights.

The standard chambering is 7.62 x 51mm NATO, but with a strong action of this type virtually any other option from .243 Winchester to .300 Winchester Magnum can be provided to order, and the barrel appropriately rifled.

Manufacturer:
Armalon, London, England

Data:

Chambering: 7.62 x 51mm NATO
Operation: Bolt action
Length: 1200mm (47.24in)
Weight: 6.60kg (14.55 lbs)
with bipod and telescope sight
Barrel:
700mm (27.56in), 4 grooves,
right-hand twist,
one turn in 280mm (11.02in)
Magazine: 5, 10 or 20 rounds
Muzzle velocity:
ca 880 m/sec (2890 ft/sec)

Milcam HB

The **Milcam** rifle is quite unique; it is the only military-grade bolt action rifle in 5.56mm calibre available. In standard form it is a very robust, simple and accurate weapon, and an ideal choice for situations where these virtues are important and an automatic weapon is not necessary. The magazine housing is to NATO standard and will accept M16 pattern magazines and those of any other NATO rifle.

The 'Cam' portion of the name of this and other rifles in the same family is due to the use of a new cam-action bolt mechanism in which rotating the handle causes cam wedges to lock the bolt into the receiver.

The **Milcam HB** is a variant on this basic model; it is still a simple and robust bolt-action rifle, but it is fitted with a slightly heavier barrel which can be rifled to either of the 5.56mm standards so that either NATO or US M193 ammunition can be used. The usual iron sights are fitted, but the top of the receiver is milled to a standard 19mm dovetail sight base to which a variety of sight mounts can be fitted, giving the user a wide option of sighting systems. The trigger mechanism also differs in having the final let-off pressure adjustable

The stock is of wood, and in the **HB** model the butt is carefully shaped with a pistol grip and cheek-rest, though no adjustments are provided. As with the standard rifle, the magazine interface will cope with any NATO standard, but a special short box is available for use when the usual 30-round curved magazine would be inconvenient.

Although standardised with a 508mm barrel, other lengths can be supplied to any reasonable requirement, as can heavier barrels.

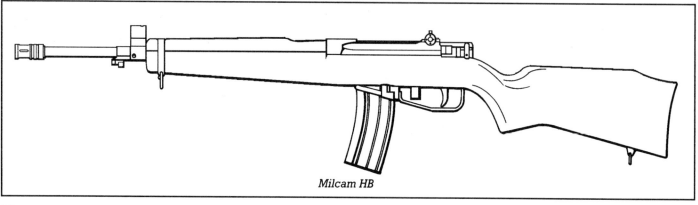

Milcam HB

The 5.56mm Milcam HB sniping rifle.

Data:

Chambering: 5.56 x 45mm
Operation: Bolt action
Length: 1050 mm (41.3 in)
Weight: 3.60 kg (7.94 lbs)
Barrel:
508mm (20 in), 6 grooves,
right-hand twist, one turn in
305mm(12in) or 178mm(7in),
depending upon ammunition to be used
Magazine: 30 round box
Muzzle velocity:
ca 950 m/sec (3115 ft/sec)

Manufacturer:
BMS Trading Ltd, London, England

Snicam

UK

Produced by the makers of the Milcam, the **Snicam** is, as the name implies, the full sniping version of the Milcam rifle. It uses the same cam-action bolt, which gives a smooth action with an angular opening and closing movement of only 22°, always an attractive feature in a sniping rifle.

The heavy barrel is free-floating in the hardwood stock, and the butt is fully adjustable for length and height of the cheek-rest. There are no iron sights, but the top of the receiver is milled into a

mounting dovetail on to which most optical and electro-optical sights can be fitted. The fore-end is fitted with a sturdy bipod having adjustable legs, and swivels are fitted to take a firing or carrying sling. A ten-shot removable box-magazine fits in place below the receiver.

Any commercial or military 5.56mm ammunition can be used, and the company offer three rifling options in order to extract the best performance. For M193 ammunition, the original

American .223 rounds, a rifling twist of one turn in 12 inches is recommended. For 5.56mm NATO rounds, using the SS109 and heavier bullets, one turn in 9 inches or one turn in seven inches, according to choice, though the 7 inch twist is recommended for use with M196 tracer ammunition. For optimum results with the Snicam rifle, the makers recommend using the Federal 69 grain bullet with the 7 or 9 inch twist.

A simpler sniping rifle offered as an alternative for police use is the 'Polcam';

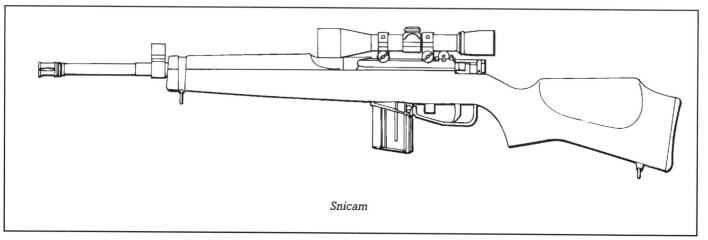

Snicam

82

The BMS Snicam rifle in firing position.

this is the same bolt action and receiver with a heavy barrel made of stainless steel and blackened. A rifling of one turn in 8.5 inches is offered with this rifle as being a pitch which will provide acceptable accuracy with almost any 5.56mm cartridge irrespective of make.

Data:

Chambering: 5.56 x 45mm
Operation: Bolt action
Length: 1194mm (47in)
Weight: 5.00 kg (11.02 lbs)
Barrel:
620mm (24.4in) , 6 grooves, right-hand twist
Magazine: 20 rounds
Muzzle velocity: 960 m/sec (3150 ft/sec)

Manufacturer:
BMS Trading Ltd, London, England

In the early 1980s the British Army began searching for a new sniping rifle to replace the elderly Lee-Enfield pattern L42 rifle which had served since the 1950s. Models were obtained from various manufacturers, and after long and exhaustive trials the 'Model PM Sniper' designed and built by Accuracy International was selected and adopted into service in 1986 as the **L96A1**.

The design of the **L96A1** caused some raised eyebrows, but arduous service has shown that the designer knew what he was doing. Instead of the traditional wooden stock, the rifle is assembled to an aluminium frame which is then surrounded by a stock made of high-impact plastic material. This form of construction ensures that the rifle remains rigid and serviceable even if the stock is damaged; provided the frame remains intact, the rifle can still be used efficiently even if all the plastic 'furniture' is removed. Furthermore, this form of construction does away with the traditional and mysterious art of 'bedding' the barrel and action into the woodwork, making maintenance and repair much easier.

The stainless steel barrel screws into an extended receiver, giving it additional support and stiffness, and a locking ring, formed with lugs, is screwed tightly against the barrel. The three bolt lugs pass through this ring and, when the bolt is turned down, lock behind the lugs. The bolt handle acts as a fourth lug as it locks into the receiver. This locking ring simplifies manufacture and, as wear

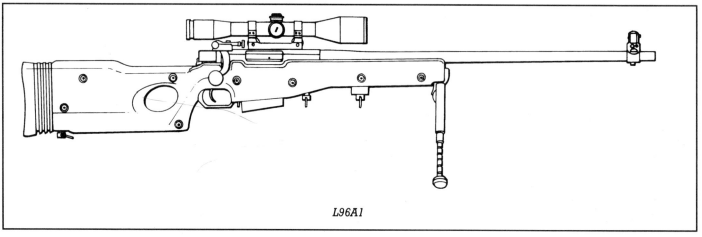

L96A1

takes place and the cartridge head clearance increases, a new ring can be fitted in a few minutes. The normal accuracy life of the barrel has been proved well in excess of 5,000 rounds.

The bolt works in a 60° arc, two-thirds of the cocking action taking place during the opening stroke and the remaining third during the closing stroke, so evening-out the effort required. The firing pin travels only 6mm to strike the cap, ensuring a fast lock time. The safety catch blocks the trigger, locks the bolt handle and blocks the firing pin, totally preventing any accidental discharge.

There is a simple and strong telescope mount which allows the sight to be removed and replaced quickly without loss of zero. The standard telescope is either a Schmidt & Bender 10 x 42 or 2.5-10x 56 zoom. Iron sights, capable of 700 metres range, are also fitted.

The **L96A1** is no longer manufactured, having been superseded by the 'second generation' Model AW described elsewhere, but it has been sold to 20 different countries and will remain in service for many years to come.

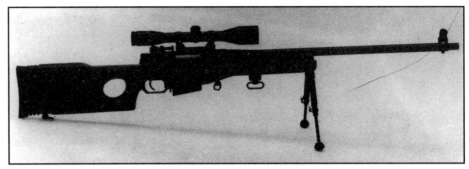

The Accuracy International 'PM' model, in its British Army L96A1 guise.

Manufacturer:
Accuracy International, Portsmouth, England

Data:

Chambering: 7.62 x 51mm NATO
Operation: Bolt action
Length: 1124mm (44.25in)
Weight: 6.50 kg (14.33 lbs)
Barrel:
655mm (25.78in), 4 grooves,
right-hand twist,
one turn in 305mm (12in)
Magazine: 10 rounds
Muzzle velocity:
ca 840 m/sec (2756 ft/sec)

Covert   UK

The company's designation for the L96A1 rifle, previously described, is the 'Model PM' and it is sold commercially under this title. A number of variations on the basic PM design were gradually developed, among them a folding butt version and a silenced version. The **'Covert'** model brings these two features together, with some other ideas, to produce a specialised sniping rifle for use in situations where a low profile is desirable.

In order to transport the **Covert** without advertising its presence, the rifle is designed to be dismantled into its major component groups and packed into a normal airline-type suitcase, complete with wheels and folding handle such as tourists use by the thousand. The silencer unit can be quickly removed, leaving the action and short barrel attached to the stock. The butt folds to the left side of the receiver, and the receiver unit, complete with telescope sight, is then fitted into the specially-shaped rubber insert inside the suitcase. The silencer unit then fits across the case diagonally. The bolt, magazine, bipod and a box of ammunition fit into their allotted spaces, the case is closed and the rifle is ready to be carried anywhere.

Assembly is simply a matter of replacing the silencer unit on to the barrel and securing it, fitting the bipod, inserting the bolt and inserting the magazine. Since the sight has not been removed from the receiver during transport there will be no need to zero the rifle or make any firing checks, so the weapon can go straight into action.

Normal ammunition can be used in the **'Covert'**, with a considerable reduction in the sound of discharge, but, of course, the bullet generates its own noise. Using subsonic ammunition reduces the muzzle report even more, and the bullet's flight is entirely silent, though the maximum effective range is somewhat reduced.

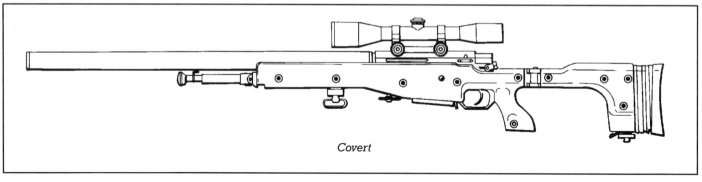

Covert

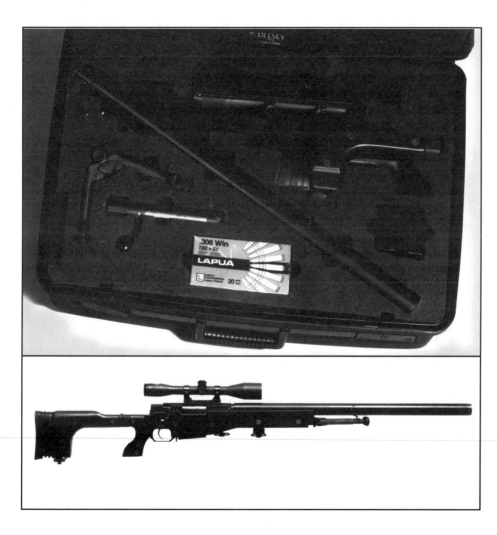

Above: The 'Covert' rifle alongside its carrying case.

Left: The 'Covert' rifle stripped and packed in its carrying case.

Below left: The Accuracy International 'Covert' silenced sniping rifle.

Data:

Chambering: 7.62 x 51mm NATO
Operation: Bolt action
Length: 1250mm (49.2in)
Weight: 6.50 kg (14.33 lbs)
Barrel: Details not available
Magazine: 10 rounds
Muzzle velocity:
ca 315 m/sec (1033 ft/sec)
(Subsonic ammunition)

Manufacturer:
Accuracy International,
Portsmouth, England

The **'Super Magnum'** generally resembles the Model AW described on page 90, but it was designed at the outset to be a superlatively accurate sniping rifle built around the .338 Lapua Magnum cartridge, with other Magnum rounds as alternative chamberings. Adopting this larger round gives the sniper more power and greater range but without increasing the size, firing signature or recoil force much beyond that of the normal 7.62 x 51mm sniping rifle, and well below the comparable effects in a .50 calibre rifle. This means a useful augmention of the sniper's powers without burdening him with excessive weight or size, and without subjecting him to discomfort or stress when firing.

The .338 Lapua Magnum cartridge (also called the 8.6 x 70mm) carries a 250-grain bullet which does not drop below the speed of sound until over 1200 metres from the muzzle, and at 1000 metres range has a striking energy of 1770 Joules (1310 foot-pounds at 1100 yards). So the weapon not only has a reliable anti-personnel capability to well beyond 1000 yards, it also has sufficient power to be a most usefully destructive round against light armour and other military equipment. The alternative calibres provide rather less performance but are nevertheless more powerful than the standard 7.62mm NATO round. Special accuracy ammunition in .338 calibre is under development in order to provide a multiple projectile capability.

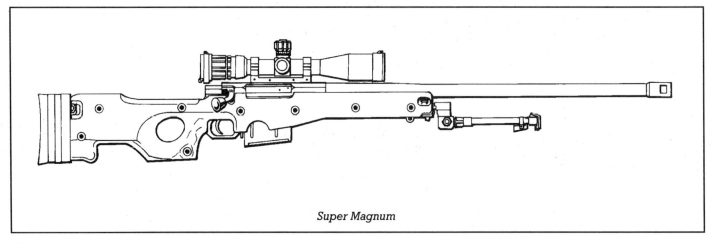

Super Magnum

An armour-piercing incendiary round, ballistically matched to the standard ball round, is already available.

The rifle uses a special heavy barrel fitted with an efficient muzzle brake, is fitted with a bipod, and has a fully adjustable shoulder stock. The standard sight is a Bausch & Lomb 10x Tactical telescope sight which has range and windage drums with 70 MOA ranging capability. Other optical and electro-optical sights could be fitted if preferred.

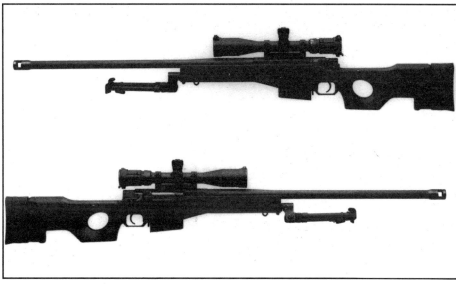

The Accuracy International 'Super Magnum' sniping rifle with Bausch & Lomb 10 x 40 telescope sight.

Data:

Chambering: .338 Lapua Magnum, .300 Winchester Magnum, or 7mm Remington Magnum
Operation: Bolt action
Length: 1268mm (49.9in)
Weight: 6.80 kg (15 lbs)
Barrel:
686mm (27in) (.338);
660mm (26in) (.300, 7mm)
Magazine:
4 (.338) or 5 (.300, 7mm) rounds
Muzzle velocity:
914 m/sec (3000 ft/sec) in .338

Manufacturer:
Accuracy International,
Portsmouth, England

89

Model AW   UK

After the British Army adopted the L96A1 rifle, Accuracy International began working on their 'second generation' model which would incorporate all the various lessons learned in the development and employment of the L96 model. At much the same time the Swedish Army set out to find a sniping rifle and rapidly decided that no off-the-shelf rifle would satisfy their requirements. In 1986 various manufacturers were advised of the Swedish specifications and invited to submit sample rifles. After two years of severe tests the Accuracy International **Model AW** (Arctic Warfare) was selected and 800 were built for Sweden as the PSG-90 sniping rifle. It has since been adopted by the Belgian Army.

The **AW rifle** maintains the basic features of the L96 design. The bolt action is the same three forward lug pattern but is easier and faster in use than the earlier model, making covert operation easier. Every component part, process and finish underwent re-evaluation with the object of arriving at a rifle which was stronger, simpler and better able to function in climatic extremes, yet easier to train on and easier to use. Endurance tests, undertaken without maintenance over 10,000 rounds, have demonstrated no noticeable wear except normal erosion of the barrel due to firing, with no failures of parts, misfeeds or malfunctions.

The **AW** has a special anti-icing bolt mechanism allowing reliable use down to -40°C, even in sudden temperature changes which cause frozen condensation. The barrel is stainless steel and is internally configured to permit firing new types of ammunition now being developed. The rifle is guaranteed to shoot inside a 20mm (3/4 inch) circle at 100 metres range, using match grade sniper ammunition, and will maintain this for several thousands of rounds.

The barrel is fitted with a muzzle brake which reduces recoil and thus facilitates spotting the fall of shot and allows quick second shots. The reduction of recoil also makes training easier and allows the

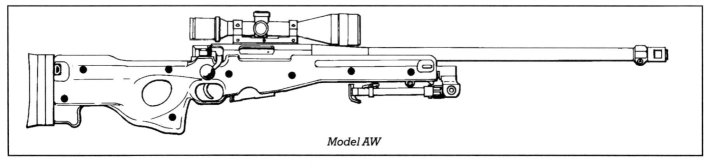

Model AW

firer better control of the rifle.

Iron sights are provided as accessories and can be quickly fitted if required. The normal sight, developed in conjunction with the rifle to meet the Swedish specification, is a Hensoldt 10 x 42 telescope sight.

A modified quick-detachable Parker-Hale bipod can be fitted, as can a firing sling, and the rifle and all its accessories

Data:

Chambering: 7.62 x 51mm NATO
Operation: Bolt action
Length: 1180mm (46.46in)
Weight: 6.10 kg (13.4lbs)
Barrel:
650mm (25.6in), 4 grooves,
right-hand twist,
one turn in 250mm (9.85in);
other twists optionally available.
Magazine: 9 or 10 rounds.
Muzzle velocity:
850 m/sec (2788 ft/sec)

Manufacturer:
Accuracy International, Portsmouth, England

Top: *The Model AW rifle complete in its aluminium transit case.*

Centre: *Accuracy International Model AW rifle with Hensoldt 10 x42 telescope.*

Bottom: *Accuracy International Model AW suppressed rifle with Schmidt & Bender 6 x42 telescope.*

Parker-Hale Model 82

The **Parker-Hale Model 82** is a bolt-action repeater using a heavy full-floating barrel of chrome-molybdenum steel with cold-forged rifling attached to a Mauser 98 bolt action. The trigger mechanism is a self-contained removable assembly which can be adjusted to provide precise trigger pull and also to compensate for wear. A triple-acting safety system locks the trigger, bolt and sear when applied. The butt is provided with spacers so that the length can be adjusted, and there is a substantial cheek-rest and recoil pad. A bipod is provided as an accessory. The result is a precision weapon which, the makers claim, gives a 99 per cent chance of a first round hit at ranges up to 400 metres in good light.

The rifle was available with various sight options; the normal iron sights were precision vernier type using a tunnel foresight, but telescope mounts were standard and a wide variety of optical and electro-optical sights can be used. For night firing, the rifle is accurate up to the extreme range of the electro-optical sight fitted.

The **Model 82** is used by three military forces; the Australian Army uses it under the title 'Rifle, 7.62mm, Sniper System' and its version is fitted with a 1200TX target rifle barrel and a Kahles Helia ZF60 telescope sight. This has a fixed 6 x 42 magnification and settings from 100 to 800 metres in 50 metre clicks. The Australian model is also slightly unusual in being fitted with precision iron sights. The same model is also in use with the New Zealand army.

The Canadian version is known as the C3 or C3A1; the C3 has the butt adjustable by spacer blocks and is also fitted with the Kahles telescope sight, but this can be removed and a vernier iron sight fitted in its place. The C3A1 has a six-shot magazine, a strengthened receiver, a bipod, and a 10x Unertl telescope sight. It is easily distinguished by the extension knob on the bolt, giving greater clearance from the telescope.

Parker-Hale no longer manufacture these rifles; the manufacturing rights were sold to Navy Arms of the USA in 1990 and, as the next entry shows, the guns are now made entirely in the USA.

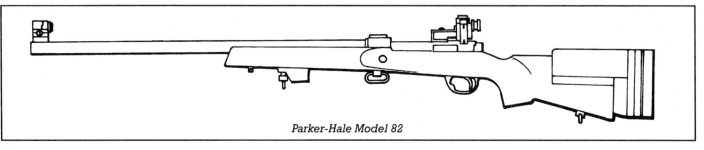

Parker-Hale Model 82

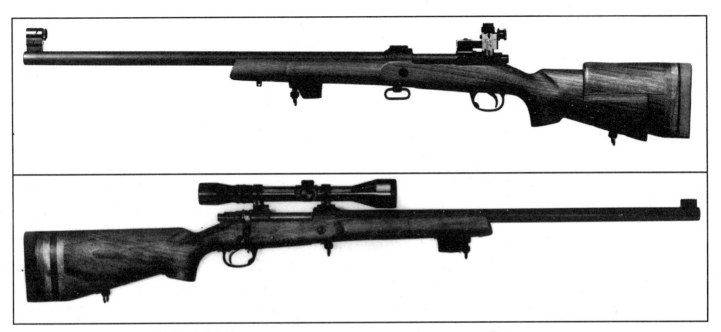

Top: Left side of the Parker-Hale Model 82 rifle, fitted with an adjustable aperture rear sight.

Above: Right side of the Parker-Hale Model 82 fitted with telescope sight.

Manufacturer:
Parker-Hale, Birmingham, England

Data:

Chambering: 7.62 x 51mm NATO
Operation: Bolt action
Length: 1162mm (45.75in)
Weight: 4.8kg (10.58 lbs)
Barrel:
660mm (26in), 4 grooves,
right-hand twist
Magazine: 4 rounds
Muzzle velocity:
ca 860 m/sec (2820 ft/sec)

Parker-Hale Model 85   USA

The Gibbs Rifle Company is a subsidiary of Navy Arms and was set up to manufacture and sell the entire range of military and sporting rifles previously made by Parker-Hale of Birmingham. Their purchase included the name, so that the Parker-Hale Model 85 is now an entirely US-made product, though it was originally designed and manufactured by Parker-Hale in Birmingham and was their last military sniping rifle design.

The **Model 85** was actually designed to compete in the trials to select a new British sniping rifle, which led to the adoption of the L96A1 (see page 84). It is a high-precision rifle, capable of 100 per cent first round hits out to 600 metres in good light. The bolt action is of the Mauser 98 type, but redesigned by Parker-Hale and provided with an oversized bolt handle based upon that developed by the Canadian Army for its **Model 82** rifle. This permits easier operation with a gloved hand, and it also places the firer's hand farther away from the sighting telescope so that there is less likelihood of upsetting the aim while reloading. An adjustable bipod is provided and is designed so

that it can be easily adjusted by the firer whilst in the firing position. Other available options include black or camouflaged stock, raised cheek piece, carrying case and all the of cleaning and maintenance accessories.

The receiver is formed with a dovetail mounting which will accept almost any optical or electro-optical sight, and also carries a built-in iron aperture sight which can be used should the telescope be damaged. The foresight is screwed on to the muzzle and retained by an Allen screw, and it can be removed so that a sound suppressor

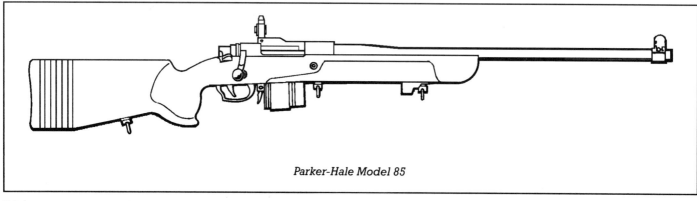

Parker-Hale Model 85

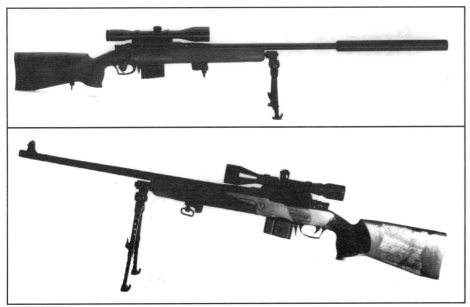

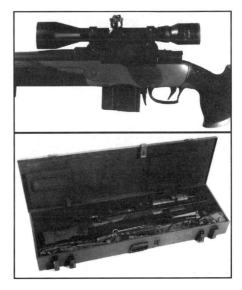

can be fitted. A mounting bracket is provided for the Simrad KN250 electro-optical sight attachment (see page 135) which permits the standard optical telescope to be used as a night sight and thus removes the need for a vertically-adjustable cheek-rest, since separate optical and electro-optical sights have different horizontal axes.

Top left: Parker-Hale M85 fitted with suppressor.

Above: Parker-Hale M85 sniper rifle.

Top right: Parker-Hale M85; close-up showing telescope and mount.

Above right: Parker-Hale M85 in transit case with accessories.

Manufacturer:
Gibbs Rifle Co Inc., Martinsburg, WV, USA

Data:

Chambering: 7.62 x 51 mm NATO
Operation: Bolt action
Length: 1150mm (45.27in)
Weight: 5.70kg (12.57lbs) with telescopic sight
Barrel: 700mm (27.56in), 4 grooves, right-hand twist,
one turn in 305mm (12in)
Magazine: 10 rounds
Muzzle velocity:
ca 880m/sec (2890ft/sec)

Rifle, Sniping, M21 USA

The US **M21** sniping rifle was originally known as the 7.62mm M14 National Match (Accurized) and has been the standard US military sniping rifle for many years, though since 1995 it is being replaced by the M24 sniping system described on page 98.

The **M21** is the basic service M14 7.62mm rifle which, more or less, was the old M1 Garand in 7.62mm calibre and with a removable 20-shot magazine. Rifles were selected during manufacture, the selection being based upon careful gauging and measurement of the barrel. The stock is of walnut, impregnated with epoxy resin to prevent water absorption and warping, and the receiver and barrel are then carefully bedded-in using a glassfibre compound. The trigger mechanism is dismantled, honed, polished, and hand-fitted to give a trigger pull between 4.4 and 4.7 lbs with a crisp release point. The gas cylinder is permanently attached to the barrel and carefully honed, and the gas piston is polished and hand-fitted to improve operation and reduce the build-up of carbon during firing. With all this done the rifle is tested and must group consistently, showing an average spread at 300 yards of not more than six inches.

The flash eliminator on the muzzle can be removed and a sound suppressor fitted; the suppressor is also carefully reamed and hand-fitted, and reduces the muzzle signature to a useful degree though without affecting the bullet's sound wave.

The normal iron sights are retained, but for sniping the weapon is fitted with a Redfield Adjustable Ranging Telescope which incorporates a rudimentary rangefinding system. The magnification zooms from 3x to 9x, and the reticle in the sight picture has two marks on the vertical line which, with the sight set at 3x, subtend 30 inches at 300 yards. Now, 30 inches is approximately the distance between a

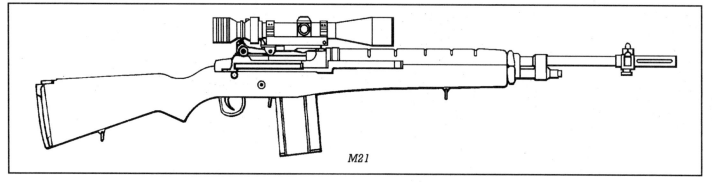

M21

Above: *The US M21 rifle uses the same mechanism as the M1 Garand of World War Two, but with a box magazine.*

Left: *Taking aim with the M21, illustrating the use of the sling.*

man's waist and the top of his helmet, so if the two marks, when laid on a man, fit his belt-buckle and helmet, he is 300 yards away. If the marks do not fit, then moving the zoom control will vary the size of the target until the marks do fit, and reading off the zoom setting will give the range in hundreds of yards. And since a ballistic cam, cut to match the characteristics of the 7.62mm cartridge, is coupled to the zoom ring, setting the range in this way also sets the telescope axis and thus sets the sight for shooting at the selected range.

Manufacturer:
Springfield Armory, Springfield, MA, USA

Data:

Chambering: 7.62 x 51mm NATO
Operation: Semi-automatic, gas
Length: 1120mm(44.1in)
Weight: 5.10 kg loaded (11.24 lbs)
Barrel:
560mm (22in), 4 grooves,
right-hand twist,
one turn in 305mm (12in).
Magazine: 20 rounds
Muzzle velocity:
ca 850 m/sec (2790 ft/sec)

In the mid-1980s the US Army decided that it would invest in a completely new sniping system, incorporating a rifle, sights, carrying case, accessories and a specially developed and manufactured ammunition, the 7.62mm M118 Special Ball round. To make things more complicated the design had to be capable of being retrofitted to adapt it to the .300 Winchester Magnum cartridge, should that cartridge be determined to be more accurate after prolonged testing and experience.

Manufacturers were notified of the requirement early in 1986, proposals had to be submitted by November 1986 and the contract was awarded in July 1987.

The winning proposal was submitted by Remington Arms. They had some experience of military sniping weapons, having provided the US Marine Corps with their M40 rifles, described on page 100, and decided that to meet this new requirement they would submit a long-action bolt-action rifle in a synthetic stock. They tested several types of stock and finally arrived at a Kevlar-graphite stock with an aluminium bedding block and an adjustable butt-plate. After this the sights, telescope sight, carrying case and other details were settled. Barrels of varying configuration were built and test-fired until a suitable design of rifling which stabilised the 173-grain bullet at all ranges was arrived at.

Once the original proposal had been accepted, the company then had to build 25 systems for First Article Testing, a

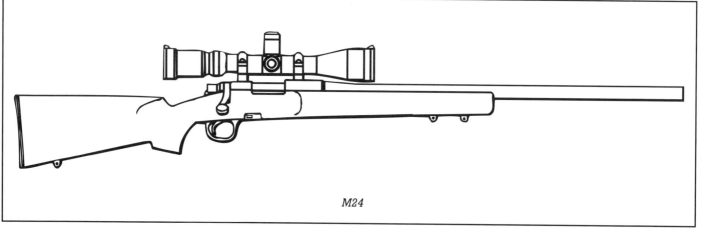

M24

stringent series of tests covering endurance, accuracy, reliability and many other features. This was passed in July 1988, and the rifle went into full production, the first 100 of a 2510-weapon order being delivered in October 1988.

The **M24** is essentially the Remington M700 rifle with a specially-rifled barrel and an M/40X custom-built trigger mechanism. The complete system consists of the rifle, bipod, laser-hardened daytime optical sight, iron sights, cleaning kit, soft rifle carrying case, telescope carrying case and total system carrying case. The complete system in its case weighs 56lbs (25.4kg).

Future additions to the system are to include the M24 Sniper Sight, a flash and blast reducing muzzle attachment, and a surveillance and spotting telescope.

The **M24** Sniping System has now been issued to Ranger and Special Forces units and infantry battalions.

Offhand firing with the US M24 sniping rifle.

Data:

Chambering: 7.62 x 51mm
Operation: Bolt action
Length: 1092mm (43in)
Weight: 5.49 kg (12.1 lbs)
Barrel: 5 grooves, right-hand twist, one turn in 285mm (11.22in)
Magazine: 6 rounds
Muzzle velocity:
ca 795 m/sec (2610 ft/sec)

Manufacturer:
Remington Arms Co, Ilion NY. USA

Rifle, M40A1 USA

In 1962 the Remington Arms Company introduced a new sporting rifle, the Model 700, which has survived to become a classic design. Chambered for innumerable cartridges, it was eventually produced in a wide variety of models to suit every conceivable requirement and purse. And among those to see what they wanted in the Model 700 was the United States Marine Corps which was looking for a sniping rifle.

The Marines have always prided themselves in their marksmanship, and even in these days of slipping standards they probably devote more time to rifle shooting skills than any other military force in existence. They retained the Springfield M1903 rifle as their sniping weapon until logistic problems with spares and repair led them to look for a replacement. The M21 used by the US Army was considered, but not for long; the Marines wanted a bolt action. A review of what was available on the commercial market brought them to the Remington 700 and, in particular the '700 Varmint' model. This was robust, simple, accurate, and available off the shelf in .308 Winchester chambering which, being the commercial equivalent of the military round, also accepts 7.62 x 51mm NATO cartridges.

Some small changes were made, principally in the matter of finish and strength; the Marines, for example, prefer a matt non-reflecting surface to a high-gloss blue finish, as might be expected.

A 10x telescope was selected and a suitable mount fitted, and the Marines had their sniping rifle; and still have.

The **M40** is a straightforward manual bolt action repeater with a long-throw bolt action and an integral magazine, though the floor plate, spring and follower can be quickly removed through the bottom of the stock for cleaning. The barrel is a special heavy pattern for stiffness and accuracy, and no iron sights are fitted. A firing sling is provided, but there is no fitting for a bipod. The **M40** must be one of the few sniping rifles in current use which does not have one. The stock is of wood, with an adjustable butt plate; in this it differs from the current commercial Model 700, which has a Kevlar-synthetic stock.

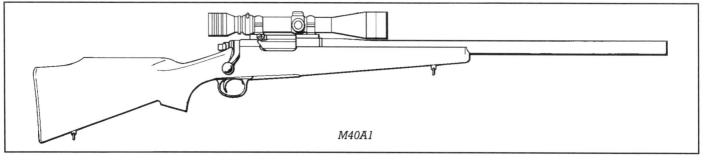

M40A1

Above: The M40A1 sniping rifle with telescope sight.
Right: Close-up of the M40A1 rifle showing the telescopic sight and the method of removing the magazine floor plate.

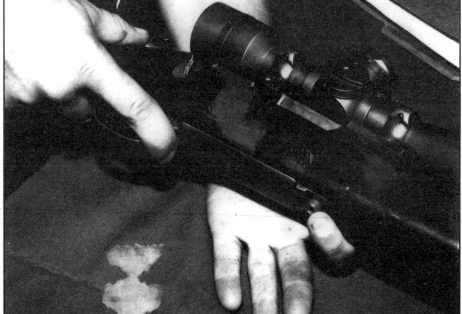

Data:

Chambering: 7.62 x 51mm NATO
Operation: Bolt action
Length: 1117mm (44in)
Weight: 6.57 kg (14.5 lbs)
Barrel:
610mm (24in), 4 grooves,
right-hand twist,
one turn in 305mm (12in).
Magazine: 5 rounds
Muzzle velocity:
ca 775 m/sec (2540 ft/sec)

Manufacturer: Remington Arms Co,
Ilion NY, USA

Grendel S-16 Silent Sniper Rifle   USA

The 5.56mm cartridge, which has rapidly become a standard infantry calibre across the world, carries the advantage of permitting a lightweight rifle. But even its best friends have to admit that the bullet does not carry much authority, and a single shot at ranges over 200 metres is not guaranteed to be fatal. Heavier bullets mean larger cartridges and bigger rifles, so the lightweight advantage goes. Or at least, it did until Grendel came along with the **S-16.**

The **S-16** is a silenced rifle based upon the well-tried M16 mechanism. Gas from behind the bullet is channelled back to impinge upon the face of the bolt carrier and drive it backwards, thus unlocking and withdrawing the rotating bolt. A spring returns the carrier and bolt, a fresh round is loaded from the magazine, the bolt closes and locks, and the weapon is ready for the next shot.

The significant difference lies in the cartridge and the barrel. Grendel have developed their own cartridge to suit the task of silent sniping out to range of 300 metres, using a bullet which will deliver a heavier blow at that range than a 9mm pistol bullet just leaving the barrel. In effect, they opened up the mouth of the normal 5.56mm cartridge case until it would take a special 14.3 gram (220 grain) streamlined bullet of 7.83mm diameter, the barrel being rifled to suit. Bullets of even greater mass were tried, but this one gives the optimum balance between accuracy and terminal energy. The propelling charge is designed to produce a muzzle velocity just below the speed of sound so that the bullet will not generate its own sound wave during flight. Muzzle blast and noise are, of

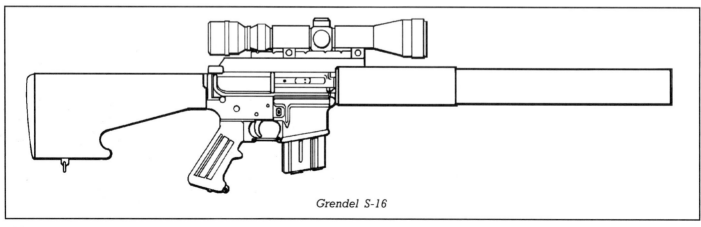

Grendel S-16

course, efficiently suppressed by the silencer unit which is integral with the barrel.

A further advantage of using the M16 as the basis for the weapon (everything other than the barrel and upper receiver are standard M16 parts) is that troops trained on the M16 need very little additional training to master the S-16, and there is also very little extra load on the maintenance and supply system.

As with most sniping weapons, no iron sights are fitted, but the receiver carries a standard sight mount base so that most types of optical and electro-optical sights can be adapted to it.

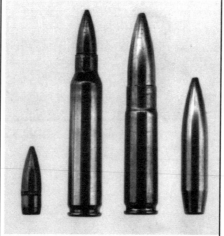

Comparison of the conventional 5.56 x 45mm bullet and cartridge (left) and the Grendel 7.62 x 36mm cartridge (right).

Data:

Chambering: 7.62 x 36mm Grendel
Operation: Gas operated, selective fire
Length: 995mm (39.2in)
Weight: 4.8kg (10.6 lbs)
with loaded magazine
Barrel: 409mm (16.1in), 6 grooves,
right-hand twist,
1 turn in 203mm (8 in)
Magazine: 20 round detachable box
Muzzle velocity:
ca 330 m/sec (1082 ft/sec)

Manufacturer:
Grendel Inc., Rockledge, Florida, USA

McMillan M93   USA

The McMillan company began, some years ago, to produce handmade hunting rifles of high quality. Seeing that the market was there, in 1986 they introduced a 7.62mm sniping rifle and in 1987 followed it with a .50 calibre weapon known as the M87. The **McMillan M93** is a revised version of their M87 model, a bolt-action repeating rifle chambered for the .50 Browning cartridge, capable of accurate shooting out to ranges in excess of 1500 yards.

The principal difference between this and the earlier weapon is the provision of a hinged butt, which can be folded around to the left of the receiver so as to make the folded weapon more convenient for carrying and stowage. Unfolded and locked into place it is absolutely rigid and no different to a fixed butt. It is, of course, adjustable for length and has an adjustable cheek-piece; it also has a useful monopod concealed inside the pistol grip

which can be extended downwards and locked so as to relieve the firer from the need to support the weight of the gun for long periods when watching for a target. There is an adjustable bipod at the front end of the stock. As an alternative, the rifle can be supplied with a one-piece glass-fibre stock which is fully adjustable for length, drop and pull.

The heavy barrel is free-floating and fitted with a high-efficiency muzzle brake which greatly reduces

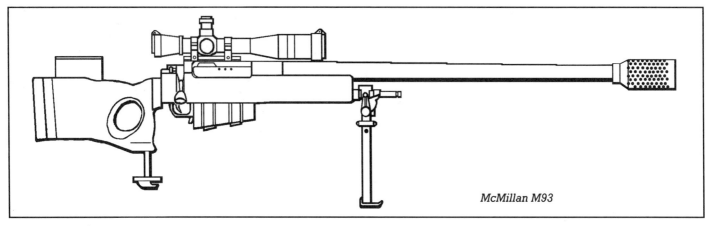

McMillan M93

the felt recoil. The removable magazine comes in two sizes and allows a skilled firer to get off between five and ten aimed rounds per minute when the need arises.

No iron sights are fitted, but the receiver is prepared for a variety of optical and electro-optical sights.

Numbers of **M93** rifles have seen service in Somalia and are currently in use in Bosnia; the French army has recently purchased 18 .

Above left: The McMillan .50 M93 heavy rifle in firing position.

Above right: The McMillan .50 M93 heavy rifle showing how the butt folds for transport.

Data:

Chambering: 12.7x99mm (.50Browning)
Operation: Bolt action
Length:
1346mm(53in) butt extended; 991mm (39in) butt folded
Weight: 9.52 kg (21 lbs)
Barrel: 737mm (29in)
Magazine: 10 or 20 rounds
Muzzle velocity:
ca 850 m/sec (2788 ft/sec)

Manufacturer:
McMillan Gun Works, Phoenix, AZ, USA

McMillan M92

The **M92** uses the same action as the M93 but breaks new ground in the .50 class by being a 'bullpup' rifle rather than one of conventional shape.

The 'bullpup' design (nobody knows where the name comes from; like Topsy, it 'just growed') involves moving the action back in the stock so that the bolt lies alongside the firer's face and the rear end of the action is virtually against the firer's shoulder - separated, of course, by some absorbent pad. The object behind this construction is to allow the greatest possible length of barrel within

a given overall length; or, as in this case, to have the same length of barrel as the conventionally-stocked rifle but reduce the overall length of the weapon by doing away with the butt-stock.

The bullpup configuration is normally found in military assault rifles, in order to have the most convenient size for rapid handling but still with the normal length of barrel. And, of course, military assault rifles today are all self-loaders, so that the soldier can settle down in a firing position and proceed to fire up to 30 rounds before he need move to

change a magazine. But with a bolt action rifle, things are a little different; there is no way that the normally constructed man can operate a bullpup bolt while remaining in the firing position, and it becomes necessary to move back from the weapon to reload. However, with a rifle of this size, there is a considerable advantage for transport and storage in having the bullpup design, and this probably outweighs the inconvenience when firing.

The action is the same front lug bolt and heavy barrel with muzzle brake, but

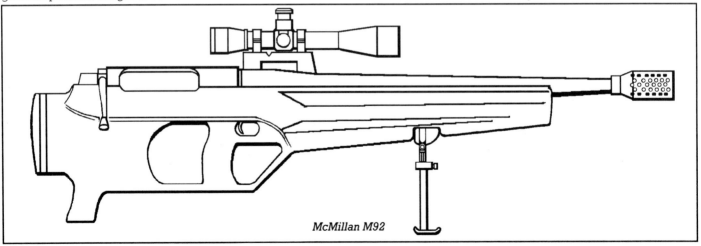

McMillan M92

The McMillan M92 'Bullpup' .50 heavy rifle in the firing position.

due to the position of the action in the stock the magazine is restricted to 5 rounds. The stock is of glass-fibre and has an adjustable cheek-piece. There is a bipod, but no rear monopod, and the usual range of optical or electro-optical sights can be fitted.

Data:

Chambering: 12.7 x 99mm (.50 Browning)
Operation: Bolt action
Length: Details not available
Weight: 10.90 kg (24 lbs) with telescope sight
Barrel: 737mm (29in)

Magazine: 5 rounds
Muzzle velocity: ca 850 m/sec (2788 ft/sec)

Manufacturer:
McMillan Gun Works, Phoenix, AZ, USA

107

Barrett M82A1 'Light Fifty' USA

The Barrett company were the first to introduce a production .50 sniping rifle, when this weapon appeared in 1983. There was a good deal of scepticism at the thought of using such a heavy weapon for sniping but, after Barrett pointed out that the object was to wreck several million dollars' worth of jet aircraft with one or two dollars' worth of cartridge, the whole thing began to make more sense and the idea spread. Since then the Barrett rifles have become the best-known of the heavy weapons and have been adopted or extensively tested by most armies. The **Light Fifty** is a semi-automatic weapon and operates by recoil. The barrel and bolt are locked together at the instant of firing, and the two are permitted to recoil back in the receiver body. The bolt is held in a separate bolt carrier, and, after the barrel assembly has moved back a short distance, this carrier is accelerated backwards at a faster speed. As it moves, so a curved cam track in the carrier, engaging with a lug on the bolt, rotates the bolt and unlocks it from the barrel. At the moment of unlocking, the barrel is halted and the carrier continues rearward, withdrawing the bolt and extracting the empty cartridge case from the chamber. The barrel is now returned to its forward position by springs, the empty case is ejected, and the bolt carrier, having compressed a spring, now stops and begins to run forward. The face of the bolt collects a cartridge from the magazine and rams it into the chamber. The bolt carrier

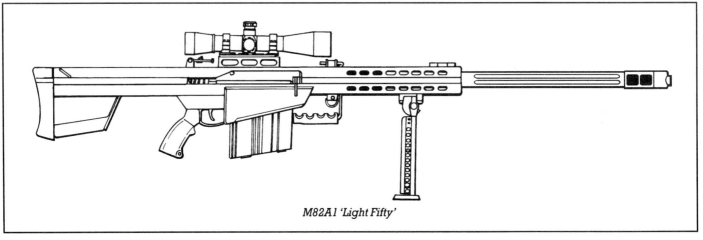

M82A1 'Light Fifty'

The Barrett M82A1 'Light Fifty' .50 heavy sniping rifle.

continues forward and now rotates the bolt into the locked position. The firing pin is cocked and held by the trigger mechanism ready for the next shot.

The heavy barrel of the rifle is fitted with a muzzle brake of 65 per cent efficiency, thus greatly reducing the felt recoil. The barrel is fluted to increase cooling area and the forward part of the receiver is perforated to allow air to circulate around the chamber. There is a bipod fitted, and the weapon can also be mounted on suitable vehicle mounts.

Iron sights are fitted for emergency use, and the receiver is prepared with a STANAG sight base capable of accepting almost any optical or electro-optical sight.

Data:

Chambering: 12.7 x 99mm (.50 Browning)
Operation: Semi-automatic, recoil
Length: 1447mm (57in)
Weight: 12.90 kg (28.44 lbs)
Barrel: 737mm (29in)
Magazine: 10 rounds
Muzzle velocity:
ca 850 m/sec (2788 ft/sec).

Manufacturer:
Barrett Firearms Mfg Co,
Murfreesboro, TN, USA

Barrett M82A2

The **M82A2** is Barrett's 'bullpup' design, though in fact the reduction in length and weight is not very great; the advantage of the bullpup layout in this case lies in the reduction of the amount of barrel stretching in front of the firer, so aiding concealment. It also makes the rifle a little more convenient to carry or stow.

The actual length of the barrel and action is the same; with a semi-automatic weapon of this power there is no possibility of reducing the recoil stroke of the bolt. Therefore the change in design has been to place the pistol grip and trigger farther forward on the receiver and put a shoulder rest just behind the magazine, leaving the bulk of the receiver, into which the bolt recoils, stretching back over the firer's shoulder. There is a forward handgrip but no bipod. The sight is placed at the front end of the receiver, with a carrying handle behind it, and iron sights are no longer fitted since the sight base would be too short for anything resembling accurate shooting. Some people have misgivings about the bullpup design, but the Barrett rifle is carefully designed so that a heavy steel plate lies between the bolt and the firer's face. Actual tests have shown that explosion of the cartridge with the bolt unlocked cannot cause an accident since the metal shielding completely protects the firer and the bolt cannot be blown out of the receiver backwards.

The Barrett rifles are excellent for the disposal of explosive devices, notably surface-laid mines, at safe distances, and for this role the Norwegian AP/HE/I round made by the Raufoss Arsenal is recommended as it disrupts the mine without detonating it.

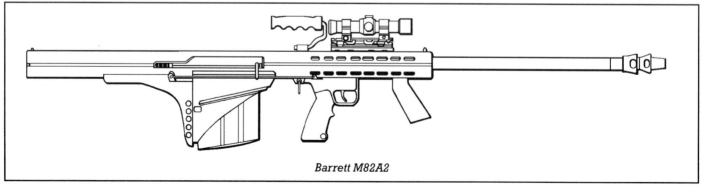

Barrett M82A2

The Barrett M82A2 is a 'Bullpup' version of the M82A1, making it rather more convenient to carry and use.

Data:

Chambering: 12.7 x 99mm
(.50 Browning)
Operation: Semi-automatic, recoil
Length: 1409mm (55.47in)
Weight: 12.24 kg (27 lbs)
Barrel: 736mm (28.97in)
Magazine: 10 rounds
Muzzle velocity:
ca 850 m/sec (2788 ft/sec)

Manufacturer:
Barrett Firearms Mfg Co,
Murfreesboro, TN, USA

Barrett M90A1

Most people begin by making a bolt-action rifle and then go on to develop a semi-automatic; Barrett reversed this method, began with the M82 semi-automatic rifle and after that had become a well-established success, developed the bolt-action **M90A1** for those people who, for one reason or another - reliability, simplicity, lightness, cheapness - prefer a manually-operated rifle.

Opportunity has been taken of the change of mechanism to make some other alterations in the design which have

resulted in a shorter, lighter and more handy weapon.

The action has been moved back in the stock, resulting in a 'bullpup' layout with the chamber alongside the firer's face and the bolt working back and forth inside the butt. The pistol grip lies in front of the magazine and a bipod is fitted to the short fore-end.

The free-floating barrel is ribbed to give additional cooling area, and is fitted with a particularly efficient muzzle brake. This, combined with the special 'Sorbathene'

shock-absorbent pad on the butt, ensures that the recoil blow felt by the firer is no worse than that of the average sporting rifle.

As with most other heavy rifles, no iron sights are fitted; there is a telescope mount on top of the receiver which will accept most commercial telescope sights, and suitable adapters allow the use of virtually any optical or electro-optical instrument.

It has been revealed that the US Navy has purchased a number of these rifles, their principal application being the long-

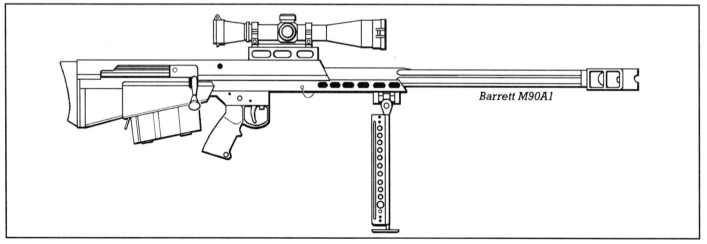

Barrett M90A1

The Barrett M90A1 bolt action rifle, simpler and lighter than the semi-automatics.

range destruction of explosive devices such as floating mines and unexploded bombs. One shot, in the right place, will generally detonate these, and firing from 500 metres or so means that the firer is well clear of any debris or fragments from the detonation.

Manufacturer:
Barrett Firearms Mfg Co,
Murfreesboro, TN, USA

Data:

Chambering: 12.7 x 99mm
(.50 Browning)
Operation: Bolt action
Length: 1143mm (45in)
Weight: 9.98 kg (22 lbs)
Barrel: 736mm (28.97in)
Magazine: 5 rounds
Muzzle velocity:
ca 850 m/sec (2788 ft/sec)

Stoner SR25

Eugene Stoner was the designer of the ArmaLite AR15 rifle and its various successors, including the M16, and he also developed a complete family of weapons under the 'Stoner-63' title, though none were ever adopted for service. One of his last designs to appear was this **SR25** rifle, which he developed for the Knight's Armament Company in the early 1990s.

The **SR25** is, in effect, the M16 rifle in 7.62mm calibre; it has also been described as a reversion to the 7.62mm ArmaLite AR-10 of forty years ago. It uses the familiar gas-actuated rotating bolt made popular by the AR15/M16 design and some 60 per cent of the component parts are completely interchangeable with the 5.56mm M16 rifle. This similarity to the M16 makes it an attractive weapon for armies already fielding the 5.56mm gun, since there will be little difficulty in training a man to use the 7.62mm version. It is understood that the US Army has shown an interest in this rifle as the combat rifle for the second man of a sniper team. His primary task is to protect the sniper, but if equipped with this rifle, it could, in an emergency, be used for the sniping tasks.

The **SR25** is not provided with sights; the receiver is flat-topped and is fitted with the US-standard 'Picatinny Rail' which is virtually the same as NATO-STANAG 2324 and will thus accept any military sight.

A number of variant models of the **SR25** have been developed. The 'Match Rifle' is a lightweight model with the flat-top receiver prepared for telescope sights. The 'Carbine' uses the same receiver but with a shorter, 406mm, barrel. The 'Sporter' is for commercial sale and resembles the M16 in having a carrying handle which is fitted with the normal M16

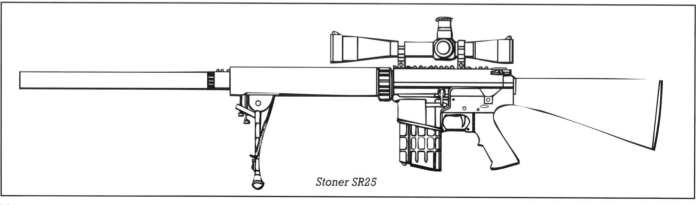

Stoner SR25

114

type of rear sight, and with the appropriate raised foresight. This can be entirely removed and replaced with a Picatinny Rail mount for fitting telescope sights. There is also a silenced version of the **SR25** with the silencer built as an integral unit with a special barrel, so that the overall length is very little more than that of the basic **SR25** rifle.

Top: The Stoner SR25 is virtually a 7.62mm version of the M16 rifle, but accurised for sniping.
***Above:** The Stoner SR25 showing the heavy barrel.*

Data:

Chambering: 7.62 x 51mm NATO
Operation: Semi-automatic, gas
Length: 117.5mm (46.28in)
Weight: 4.88 kg (10.75 lbs)
Barrel: 506mm (20 inches)
Magazine: 10 or 20 rounds
Muzzle velocity:
ca 880 m/sec (2885 ft/sec)

Manufacturer:
Knight's Armament Co, Vero Beach, FL, USA

Ruger M77 Mark II Police Rifle USA

Sturm, Ruger & Company introduced their **Model 77** rifle in 1968 and in subsequent years the design was refined, produced in a wide variety of calibres, and expanded to include various models aimed at specific types of sportsmen. They gained a sound reputation for reliability and accuracy, as a result of which numbers of police forces began employing them as sniping rifles. In 1989 the **Model 77 Mark II** rifle appeared; this had an improved trigger and a new three-position safety system; the extractor was a fixed blade, and a patented magazine floor-plate release catch was set into the trigger-guard.

Among the various models produced was the Model 77V 'Varmint' with a heavy barrel, and this has been used as the starting point for the Police Rifle.

The Police Rifle is seen primarily as a counter-sniper weapon. It uses a standard Mauser-pattern bolt action with dual opposed front locking lugs and a fixed extractor. The heavy barrel is hammer-forged stainless steel and the action body is heat-treated, investment-cast chrome-molybdenum steel. The barrel is free-floating in the American black hardwood stock. A Harris detachable pivoting bipod is provided as standard, together with a firing sling

and cleaning equipment.

The three-position safety, when in its rear position, locks the bolt and prevents firing; in the central position the gun still cannot fire, though the bolt can be opened; and in the forward position both bolt and trigger are free to move. The magazine capacity has been reduced from the usual five rounds to four in order to permit a more slender contour of the stock around the action.

The rifle is normally supplied chambered for the 7.62 x 51mm (.308 Winchester) cartridge; a 5.56 x 45mm version is also available, and the rifle can be chambered for virtually any suitable

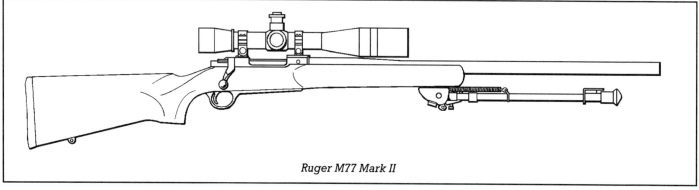

Ruger M77 Mark II

Above: The Ruger M77 Mark II Police Rifle with bipod folded.

Right: The triple safety catch and bolt of the Ruger M77 Mark II rifle.

medium-calibre cartridge desired. When firing good quality 7.62mm ammunition, one-inch groups at 100 yards are normal.

No iron sights are fitted, but the rifle is supplied with commercial one-inch telescope rings and a dovetail mount is machined into the receiver.

Data:

Chambering: 7.62 x 51mm NATO
Operation: Bolt action repeater
Length: 1184mm (46.6in)
Weight: 4.42 kg (9.75 lbs)
Barrel: 660 mm (26in), 6 grooves, right-hand twist, one turn in 254mm (10in).
Magazine: 4 rounds
Muzzle velocity:
ca 880 m/sec (2885 ft/sec)

Manufacturer:
Sturm, Ruger & Co., Southport, CT, USA

AMMUNITION

The descriptive notes which follow are based upon the standard issue ball cartridge. 'Match Grade' ammunition is invariably specified by rifle manufacturers as being the best for their particular product, but unfortunately there is no firm definition of what 'Match Grade' really means. In general, it can be taken to mean ammunition which has been specially processed so that all bullets have been checked for concentricity and weight, that tighter tolerances have been applied to the weights of bullet and charge, that the cartridge cases have been selected from a single batch so that all have the same cubic capacity and dimensions, and that the assembly has been carefully checked for bullet intrusion, bullet pull, cap depth and security and similar points.

5.56 x 45mm NATO

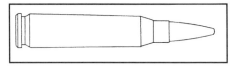

This is the cartridge which emerged from the 1978-81 NATO Small Arms Trial as the winner for the position of standard NATO infantry rifle round. Although there were a number of exotic contestants, it was fairly obvious from the start that the 5.56mm cartridge would be selected: the Americans had unilaterally adopted it as their infantry round, several nations had begun manufacturing rifles in this calibre and there was a considerable amount of money invested in ammunition production. But instead of simply rubber-stamping the American round, the trials went into great detail and eventually selected the SS109 round developed by FN Herstal. This uses a somewhat heavier bullet than the original American round and launches it at a slightly lower velocity, but its downrange performance is better due to its better carrying power

Overall Length: 57.3mm (2.256in)
Case Length: 44.45mm (1.75in)
Rim diameter: 9.50mm (.374in)
Bullet weight: 4.00g (62 grains)
Muzzle velocity: 930m/sec (3051 ft/sec)
Muzzle energy: 1708J (1264 ft/lbs)
Velocity at 300 metres:
650 m/sec (2133 ft/sec)
Energy at 300 metres: 834J (617 ft/lbs)

5.56 x 45mm M193

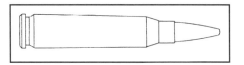

This is the 'original' .223 cartridge developed with the AR15/M16 rifle from a commercial Winchester round. It caused something of a furore after its introduction, with wild and wonderful tales of how it 'tumbled in flight' so as to produce incredible wounds, though nobody ever explained how it managed to fly accurately if it tumbled in flight. It was marginally stable, fired from rifling with one turn in 12 inches, and the bullet certainly tended to topple once it struck and did develop severe wounds, but most of the damage, it was later ascertained, was from bullet break-up due to the high velocity. But the reputation stuck, so much that the Swedes insisted on a faster turn of rifling so as to make it less dangerous. Its supersession by the SS109 round for the NATO standard was due to the better penetration performance at longer ranges of the heavier Belgian bullet.

Overall Length: 57.3mm (2.256in)
Case Length: 44.45mm (1.75in)
Rim diameter: 9.50mm (.374in)
Bullet weight: 3.63g (56 grains)
Muzzle velocity:
975 m/sec (3200 ft/sec)
Muzzle energy: 1692J (1252 ft/lbs)
Velocity at 300 metres:
626 m/sec (2054 ft/sec)
Energy at 300 metres: 698J (517 ft/lbs)

.243 Winchester

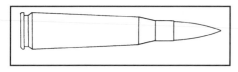

The .243 Winchester is a commercial round which has been adopted by some makers of sniping rifles because of its outstanding accuracy allied to a low recoil force when compared to larger calibre rounds. It appeared in 1955, and was originally developed by taking the 7.62 x 51mm NATO cartridge case and reducing the neck diameter to accept a 6mm bullet. In practice, this means that any weapon designed for the 7.62mm NATO round can be fairly readily adapted to .243 by changing the barrel; the remainder of the weapon will not need much alteration.

Overall Length: 68.8mm (2.709in)
Case Length: 51.9mm (2.043in)
Rim diameter: 12.0mm (.472in)
Bullet weight: 6.48g (95 grains)
Muzzle velocity:
836 m/sec (2743 ft/sec)
Muzzle energy: 2257J (1670 ft/lbs)
Velocity at 300 metres:
631 m/sec (2070 ft/sec)
Energy at 300 metres: 1285J (951 ft/lbs)

7mm Remington Magnum

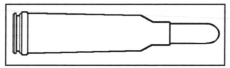

Another commercial hunting cartridge adopted for sniping because of its accuracy, the 7mm Remington Magnum appeared in 1962 to accompany a new range of bolt-action hunting rifles. It was the first belted cartridge to appear from a major manufacturer for many years. Belted magnum rounds from small makers and 'wildcat' developers had become popular, and Remington saw a market niche which they promptly exploited. The benefits of a belted case lie principally in the very positive location of the case in the chamber, leading to consistent ballistic conditions, and the strength of the case body in the belt area which permits the use of magnum loadings with no danger of stretched or burst cases.

Overall length: 82.30mm (3.24in)
Case Length: 63.5mm (2.50in)
Rim diameter: 13.33mm (.525in)
Bullet weight: 9.72g (150 grains)
Muzzle velocity:
948 m/sec (3110 ft/sec)
Muzzle energy: 4358J (3225 ft/lbs)
Velocity at 300 metres:
686 m/sec (2250 ft/sec)
Energy at 300 metres:
2282J (1689 ft/lbs)

7.5mm French Service

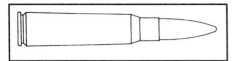

This cartridge is only found in one or two rifles adopted by, or hoping to be adopted by, the French Army, because nobody else uses this cartridge. The 7.5mm was probably the last of the old-style full-power cartridges to be designed; the French finished World War One without a decent light machine gun, and wisely saw that their first priority was a rimless cartridge case, since their 1886 8mm Lebel cartridge used a wide rim and a very sharply tapered body which drove machine gun feed engineers into hysterics. After attempting to re-invent the 7.92mm Mauser, they then adopted the 7.5mm Swiss as their model and produced this round in 1929. It served them well, but the French have now almost given it up, retaining it only for a handful of sniping rifles - most of their 7.5mm weapons now being either obsolete or converted to 7.62mm NATO calibre.

Overall Length: 75.95mm (2.99in)
Case Length: 53.59mm (2.11in)
Rim diameter: 12.24mm (.482in)
Bullet weight: 12.31g (190 grains)
Muzzle velocity:
835 m/sec (2740 ft/sec)
Muzzle energy: 3138J (2322 ft/lbs)
Velocity at 300 metres:
568 m/sec (1863 ft/sec)
Energy at 300 metres:
1452J (1074 ft/lbs)

.300 Winchester Magnum

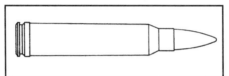

Another cartridge with a belted case and the emotive title 'Magnum'. It appeared in 1963 and, like the 7mm Remington Magnum, was calculated to replace the many small-quantity and wildcat cartridges using belted cases that had become popular. Its first appearance in the quasi-military field was its adoption by Walther for their short-lived WA2000 sniping rifle in the late 1970s. They chose it because extensive tests showed that it was more accurate than anything else in that particular rifle, which was, by any measure - quality or price - the 'Rolls-Royce' of sniping rifles. It proved to be too much of a good thing for the market, however, and vanished. But others have followed Walther's lead and selected the .300 Winchester Magnum cartridge for sniping purposes because of its accuracy; the only thing which held it back from military use was the lack of a full-jacketed bullet, but this was eventually provided and the round is gaining more devotees every year.

Overall Length: 83.82mm (3.30in)
Case Length: 66.55mm (2.62in)
Rim diameter: 13.51mm (.532in)
Bullet weight: 9.72g (150 grains)
Muzzle velocity: 987m/sec (3238 ft/sec)
Muzzle energy: 4725J (3496 ft/lbs)
Velocity at 300 metres:
693 m/sec (2274 ft/sec)
Energy at 300 metres:
2329J (1723 ft/lbs)

7.62 x 36mm Grendel

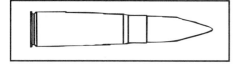

This highly specialised cartridge is manufactured by Grendel for their silent sniper rifle and is essentially the 5.56mm M193 case shortened and with the neck opened out to take a 7.62mm bullet. Very little has been disclosed about it, but it is claimed that the extremely high ballistic coefficient of the streamlined bullet allows it to retain more energy at 300 metres than a standard 9mm bullet fired from a submachine gun has at the muzzle.

Overall Length: 55mm (2.165in)
Case Length: 36mm (1.417in)
Rim diameter: 9.5mm (.374in)
Bullet weight: 14.3g (220 grains)
Muzzle velocity:
ca. 330 m/sec (1082 ft/sec)
Muzzle energy: ca. 778J (575 ft/lbs)
Velocity at 300 metres: Not divulged
Energy at 300 metres: Not divulged

7.62 x 51mm NATO

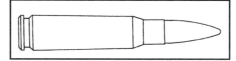

NATO's standard from the 1950s to the 1980s, this first saw the light of day as the American T65, a compromise put forward in opposition to the British 7mm (.280) round in the early 1950s. At that time the idea of a short cartridge and lighter rifle held no appeal for the US Army, whilst the rest of NATO balked at the full-power .30-06 Springfield cartridge. The compromise was reached by shortening the .30-06 case and putting a lighter bullet in it, ending up with a round which was neither full-power nor 'compact', and putting paid to any European ideas of adopting short assault rifles for several years. As cartridges go, it wasn't bad, but it took a good deal of hard work in the ammunition factories before it managed to gain a reputation for accuracy.

Overall Length: 69.85mm (2.75in)
Case Length: 51.05mm (2.01in)
Rim diameter: 11.94mm (.470in)
Bullet weight: 9.65g (149 grains)
Muzzle velocity: 854 m/sec (2802 ft/sec)
Muzzle energy: 3519 J (2604 ft/lbs)
Velocity at 300 metres:
642 m/sec (2106 ft/sec)
Energy at 300 metres:
1988 J (1471 ft/lbs)

7.62 x 54R Soviet

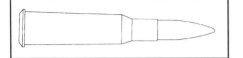

One of the oldest cartridges still in regular use, this first appeared when the Tsar's army adopted the Mosin-Nagant rifle in 1891. Rimmed and sharply tapered, it looks its age, but as a full-powered long-range round it yields place to nobody in its calibre group and the Russians knew what they were doing when they designed the Dragunov rifle to fire it.

Overall Length: 76.70mm (3.020in)
Case Length: 53.60mm (2.110in)
Rim diameter: 14.30mm (.563in)
Bullet weight: 11.98g (185 grains)
Muzzle velocity:
804 m/sec (2638 ft/sec)
Muzzle energy: 3814J (2822 ft/lbs)
Velocity at 300 metres:
 606 m/sec (1988 ft/sec)
Energy at 300 metres:
2167J (1603 ft/lbs)

7.92 x 57mm Mauser

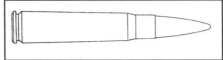

Another venerable veteran, first introduced in 1888 and one of the most popular military rifle cartridges ever made. It was also widely used as a sporting round (generally under the title 8 x 57mm to set it apart from its military employment) and collectors can have a merry time with it since it has appeared with just about every bullet known to man. For consistency and accuracy there are few military rounds to beat it, and its survival as a sniping round is not surprising. And, of course, like all military cartridges of its era, it carries its authority well downrange; 1500 foot-pounds of energy at 300 yards means that whatever gets hit, stays hit. Even at 1000 yards energy is still over 200 ft/lbs, four times the amount generally considered necessary to give a knockdown blow.

Overall Length: 80.60mm (3.173in)
Case Length: 57.00mm (2.244in)
Rim diameter: 12.0mm (.472in)
Bullet weight: 12.85g (198 grains)
Muzzle velocity:
737 m/sec (2418 ft/sec)
Muzzle energy: 3490J (2582 ft/lbs)
Velocity at 300 metres:
554 m/sec (1818 ft/sec)
Energy at 300 metres:
1972J (1460 ft/lbs)

.338 Lapua Magnum

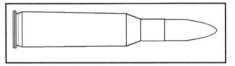

This cartridge was specially developed by Lapua to produce the most accurate and reliable hunting round possible. Having done that, its application to sniping was obvious and quickly followed. It was derived from the existing .416 Rigby cartridge case, shortened and with the neck diameter reduced to take the new .338 bullet. The combination of heavy bullet and high velocity means long-ranging energy - at 2000 yards this bullet is still carrying 463 foot-pounds.

Overall Length: 91.50mm (3.602in)
Case Length: 69.20mm (2.724in)
Rim diameter: 14.91mm (.587in)
Bullet weight: 16.20g (250 grains)
Muzzle velocity:
914 m/sec (3000 ft/sec)
Muzzle energy: 6766J (5007 ft/lbs)
Velocity at 300 metres:
763 m/sec (2503 ft/sec)
Energy at 300 metres:
4710J (3485 ft/lbs)

9 x 39mm Soviet

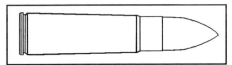

This is an entirely new Russian cartridge about which not everything is yet known. It has been arrived at by opening out the standard 7.62 x 39mm cartridge case and providing it with a new bullet. The bullet weight and charge have been selected in order to produce a subsonic round suitable for use in various silent weapons, including the VSS Silent Sniper. Two rounds are known; a ball round using a composite bullet with a part lead, part steel core and retaining an airspace at the tip of the core so as

to permit the bullet tip to deform on impact and thus give greater terminal effect against personnel; and an armour-piercing round containing a hard steel core which protrudes through the tip of the bullet jacket. In view of the velocity and energy figures, we must assume that any armour piercing capability will be demonstrated at fairly short ranges against fairly thin armour.

Overall Length: 55.5mm (2.185in)
Case Length: 38.5mm (1.516in)
Rim diameter: 11.3mm (.445in)
Bullet diameter: 9.20mm (.362in)
Bullet weight: 16.2g (250grains)
Muzzle velocity: 290 m/sec (951 ft/sec)
Muzzle energy: 681J (503 ft/lbs)

.50 Browning

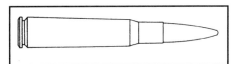

The history of this remarkable cartridge starts in 1918 when General Pershing called for a heavy anti-aircraft machine gun. The war ended before much was done, but in1919 an enlarged Browning machine gun had been developed and this cartridge

was designed by simply scaling-up the existing .30 Model 1906 rifle cartridge. It came into its own during World War Two, and, after 1945, the gun and cartridge were adopted by almost every nation outside the orbit of the Soviet Union. By remarkable applications of technology the ammunition is still holding its place, even though its demise has been forecast for some years; every attempt to supplant it by a fresh design of machine gun and cartridge has failed, largely due to the vast numbers of guns in use, a quantity which would be expensive to replace. The adoption of the cartridge for use in heavy anti-materiel rifles can only extend its life even further.

Overall Length:
137.80mm (5.425in)
Case Length: 99.10mm (3.90in)
Rim diameter: 20.30mm (.800in)
Bullet weight: 42.90g (662 grains)
Muzzle velocity:
887 m/sec (2910 ft/sec)
Muzzle energy:
16,876J (12,488 ft/lbs)
Velocity at 300 metres:
665 m/sec (2182 ft/sec)
Energy at 300 metres:
9476J (7012 ft/lbs)

12.7 x 107 Soviet

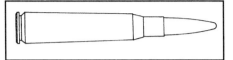

This might be said to be the Soviet answer to the .50 Browning, being of similar shape, size and performance. It was developed in the late 1920s and is said to have leaned upon the German 13mm Tank und Flieger cartridge under development in 1918, for much of its inspiration, though it might equally well have been based upon the Browning round. It was first used with the Degtyarev DK heavy machine gun in the mid-1930s and then in the modified DShK guns, and has remained in use ever since. It has been widely distributed to the many countries under Soviet influence in the postwar years and made under licence in China and the Middle East. With the American pioneering in heavy rifles using the .50 Browning, it is hardly surprising that similar designs adapted to this cartridge have appeared in countries in which it is a common round. So far as performance in rifles is concerned we have little solid information, but it should be on a

par, both for accuracy and destructive power, with the Browning round.

Overall Length: 146.8mm (5.780in)
Case Length: 105.9mm (4.169)
Rim diameter: 21.6mm (.850in)
Bullet weigh: 48.28g (745 grains)
Muzzle velocity: 840 m/sec (2756 ft/sec)
Muzzle energy: 15,570J (11,522 ft/lbs)
Velocity at 300 metres:
630 m/sec (2067 ft/sec)
Energy at 300 metres:
9572J (7083 ft/lbs)

14.5 x 114mm Soviet

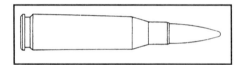

Once the 12.7mm Soviet round had appeared in a rifle it was only a matter of time before this 14.5mm cartridge was tried in the same role. This monster was devised as an anti-tank rifle cartridge and it certainly fuelled the most potent of all the World War Two anti-tank rifles, the Russians using them long after everyone else had abandoned them. After the war its performance was too good to lose, and the KPV heavy machine gun was built

around it, proving to be a useful air defence weapon. The steel-cored armour-piercing bullet can go through 28mm of armour at 300 metres range and the figures below indicate that it will retain quite adequate power to deal with light armour well downrange. There are also AP/Incendiary bullets, and a high explosive incendiary which can go through duralumin plate at 1500 metres and ignite a fuel tank behind it. But with a 63 gram bullet leaving the barrel at 3200 feet a second, you need a fairly substantial shoulder against the butt.

Overall Length: 156mm (6.142in)
Case Length: 114.3mm (4.50in)
Rim diameter: 26.9mm (1.059in)
Bullet weight: 63.44g (980 grains)
Muzzle velocity: 976 m/sec (3200 ft/sec)
Muzzle energy: 30,215J (22,360 ft/lbs)
Velocity at 300 metres:
732 m/sec (2402 ft/sec)
Energy at 300 metres:
16,979 J (12,565 ft/lbs)

15.2mm Steyr

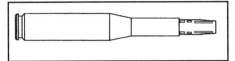

This is strictly a one-weapon cartridge, having been under development since 1988 by Steyr-Mannlicher for their AMR heavy anti-materiel rifle. It originally appeared in 15mm calibre, then changed to 14.5mm and has now settled at 15.2mm. The projectile is an arrow-like fin-stabilised tungsten dart which can pierce 40mm of steel armour at 800 metres range and deliver sufficient secondary fragmentation behind the armour to do severe damage to whatever the armour was protecting. The cartridge case uses a metal base and synthetic body and is generally conventional in its bottle-necked form. A long primer extends well into the case to give optimum ignition of the charge, and a pusher plate behind the dart drives it up the bore. The dart is stabilised in the bore by a light plastic sabot which discards at the muzzle.

Overall Length: 207mm (8.149in)
Case Length: 169mm (6.654in)
Rim diameter: 26mm (1.02in)
Bullet weight: 35g (540 grains)
Muzzle velocity:
1450 m/sec (4757 ft/sec)
Muzzle energy: 36,793J (27,227 ft/lbs)
Velocity at 300 metres: Not divulged
Energy at 300 metres: Not divulged

---

20 x 82mm MG151

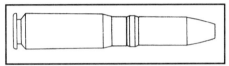

This cartridge was developed in the late 1930s for use with a Mauser aircraft cannon known as the MG151. This began life as a 15mm machine gun, but was later enlarged to 20mm at the request of the Luftwaffe. It was also used by the Japanese Air Force, and after 1945 the French Air Force adopted it. The French in turn sold aircraft with these guns to various countries, and thus the cartridge spread around the world. By the 1970s it was generally considered obsolescent, but it had a revival in South Africa in the 1980s. The South African cartridge actually has some minute dimensional differences to the original Mauser design, but still functions in all MG151-type weapons. It was this South African restoration which led to the Aerotek company adopting it for their heavy rifle; it is the least powerful of existing 20mm cartridges and possibly the only one adaptable to off-the-shoulder rifles. An advantage is that the available projectile types include inert ball, high explosive, high explosive/ incendiary, armour piercing, armour piercing/incendiary and practice, all with the option of tracer, a selection which makes the anti-materiel role of the Aerotek rifle a comprehensive one.

Overall Length: 147mm (5.787in)
Case Length: 81.7mm (3.216in)
Rim diameter: 25.1mm (0.988in)
Bullet weight: 110g (1697 grains)
Muzzle velocity:
720 m/sec (2362 ft/sec)
Muzzle energy: 28,500J (21,080 ft/lbs)
Velocity at 300 metres:
540 m/sec (1772 ft/sec)
Energy at 300 metres:
16,022J (11,856 ft/lbs)

SIGHTS AND ACCESSORIES

Except for shotguns, no firearms are of much use without sights, and the more precise the shooting, the more important and complicated will be the sights. That being the case, you might expect that sniping rifles would be fitted with the same sort of sights as target rifles, but it is not quite as simple as that.

Iron sights (or open sights), metal components attached to the rifle, come in various forms. Perhaps the most common is a vertical blade foresight and a vee-shaped backsight; alternatively, the backsight might have a U-shaped notch or a square notch. In all these the requirement is to place the foresight centrally in the notch and level with the top of the notched surface. For the utmost precision, the U or square notch is generally considered superior to the vee, but sporting shooters prefer the vee because it gives them better visibility of the target's immediate surroundings, and it also makes following a moving target easier.

Aligning foresight, backsight and target demand that all three items be in focus, a skill which is not possible for everyone and which tends to diminish with age. Moreover, aligning them accurately is something which takes a good deal of training and practice. As a result of this the aperture backsight has generally replaced the open notch backsight, certainly for military rifles. Here the firer has to place the tip of the foresight in the centre of the aperture, and this is a skill which is inherently easier than centralising and levelling it in a notch, so that training recruits becomes quicker and easier.

There are also mechanical advantages; if the rearsight is close to the eye it can be small, so making the sighting more precise, and the smallness of the aperture aids in the focusing, very much in the same manner that stopping down a camera lens to a smaller aperture improves the depth of field in focus. On the other side of the scale the aperture restricts the amount of light reaching the eye, and it effectively prevents the shooter

seeing much of the target's surroundings. Target shooters go further and use an aperture foresight as well, and while this can be superlatively accurate in skilled hands, it is out of the question for military use, since it is far too slow to pick up a target and virtually impossible to take snap shots or follow a moving target; it also demands far longer training and practice than any other kind of sight.

The aperture also tends to show deficiencies when the light is poor. The small aperture which aids focusing restricts the amount of light to the point that open-notch sights can be used in light which is too poor for an aperture. This can be redressed by having a larger aperture, and, again, target sights frequently have a series of different-sized apertures which can be slipped or revolved into position until the shooter finds one which suits the light, the range and everything else. Again, wonderfully accurate but too complex and time-consuming for military use.

But, you say, the sniper can take his time, fiddle with sights, adjust things

A typical sighting telescope; a Schmidt & Bender 3x to 12x zoom telescope mounted on an Accuracy International Model AWP rifle.

to a nicety before he fires. Well, yes and no; sometimes he can, more often he cannot. Fiddling with sights means movement, and movement can betray him. He may have but a fleeting opportunity to shoot, even though he may have lain for hours awaiting that opportunity. When the target presents itself he must aim accurately and shoot quickly, and be prepared for a second shot if necessary and possible. The simpler the sight, the better; instead of worrying about sight settings and choice of apertures he can devote his attention to his target.

The dictionary definition of sniping is 'To fire shots from hiding, especially at long range', and once we begin to look at long range shooting the iron sight is even less attractive. Indeed, some sights can obscure a standing man at 1000 yards with the foresight blade. And so the obvious answer was to look at a telescope; if an ordinary telescope can bring objects closer and render them clearer, then attaching a telescope to a gun should do the same thing for the sights.

The use of a telescope as a rifle sight goes back a long way; a description can be found in *Magister Naturae et Artis* by Francesco de Lana, published in 1684. And in 1702 a manual called *Oculus Artificialis Teledioptricus* describes a rifle sight with four lenses and a glass disc with an engraved centre spot to act as the aiming mark. Frederick the Great recorded shooting with a telescope sighted rifle in his diary in 1737. Telescope sights are believed to have been used to a very limited extent during the American War of Independence, but the first major military application came in the American Civil War when members of the various regiments of sharpshooters began using heavy-barrelled target rifles with telescopes. These, due to the limitations of optical technology, were usually long and with small-diameter lenses, giving a dark and indistinct sight picture by modern standards, but by the standards of their day they were a major advance on iron sights and they allowed precise shooting at ranges well outside the capability of iron sights.

What soon became apparent was that such sights were delicate instruments, and that they were likely to go out of adjustment fairly rapidly under the hammering of the rifle's recoil. This was particularly likely if there was any looseness or play in the mounting of the telescope to the rifle; the sudden movement of the rifle as the shot was fired would be resisted by the inertia of the telescope and cause it to slip in its mounting, thus becoming inaccurate and, over a period of time, so battering the interface that accuracy became impossible. And, of course, the sudden and violent acceleration of the telescope often caused lenses and other parts to loosen and go out of adjustment. Even so, provided a repair system could be organised, and provided spare sights were available, the telescope can be said to have paid its way and made its mark on the battlefield.

The First World War simply saw the existing technology brought out, dusted, and put into play once more. Again, the robustness of the sight and

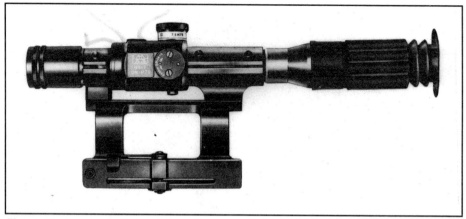

Above: The Russian PSO-1 sighting telescope used with the Dragunov rifle.

its mounting became prime problem areas, and the war years saw much advance in developing robust telescopes and efficient mountings. Parallel with this, of course, telescope sights for hunting had become common from the 1890s onwards, and much work had been put into these same questions of robustness and resistance to shock, particularly when the telescope was mounted on some major-calibre big game rifle.

However, the most sudden advance in telescope sights came in the 1960-70 period with the arrival of computer-designed lenses.

Hitherto, lenses had to be designed by mathematical formulae, using seven figure logarithms and hand calculators, and it was a long and slow business. Having designed the lens, it had to be ground and tested; if the results were not as expected, then the design had to be gone through again and another model ground. But computer design and modelling allows a complex lens to be designed in half a day and tested on a computer model, redesigned if necessary, and then the formula handed to a computer-controlled grinding machine which runs up the lens in a matter of hours to an

A Swiss Kern telescope mounted on the Swiss Army StuG90 rifle.

accuracy only previously achieved by a handful of technicians in weeks of work. This brought the cost of telescopes down with a rush, and it allowed designers to concentrate upon construction and robustness, so that today it is possible to walk into any gunsmith and emerge with a telescope which will outperform anything made fifty years ago.

One of the principal advantages of the telescope is that it gathers far more light than the naked eye, and, therefore, the picture of the target is brighter than that seen over iron sights. This has particular significance at dawn and dusk; the sniper with a telescope will be able to open fire earlier and keep firing later than his companion with an iron-sighted weapon. It is for this reason that the terms 'First Telescope Light' and 'Last Telescope Light' came into use in the British Army, indicating the times that optically-aided weapons can be expected to have an advantage over conventionally-sighted ones.

The telescope sight that everybody knows is more correctly described as a 'terrestrial telescope'. It is in a tube with a lens at one end, an eyepiece at the other, and what goes in between is the business of the maker and what he thinks is appropriate. But there is another type of sighting telescope which is very little known - the Galilean telescope. At its most elementary this consists of two lenses, one at the muzzle of the rifle and the other on the breech end in some convenient place for the firer to apply his eye. In front of the rear lens there is a plate with an aperture in it, and marked on the front lens is an aiming mark. Now you may think that with two lenses out in the open you are not going to see very much, but it works. It was used many years ago by target shooters but was abandoned because of certain optical defects which meant that you could have the aiming mark in sharp focus, or you could have the target in sharp focus, but you couldn't have both in sharp focus at the same time. So you made up your mind which you wanted sharp and which you were satisfied to have fuzzy, and did the best you could. When the terrestrial telescope was perfected as a rifle sight, the Galilean was more or less abandoned.

It came back in the 1980s, by way of Israel, and modern optical technology has got rid of the drawbacks which bedevilled it in years gone by. It now calls itself a 'head-up display' but the setup is entirely the same. It has considerable advantages for fast shooting; the firer can aim with both eyes open, he has full peripheral vision around the target, and so long as he puts the aiming mark on the target it does not matter where his eye is in

The return of the Galilean telescope; the Elbit 'Falcon' sight from Israel mounted on a Galil rifle. The front lens is easily seen; the rear lens and aperture are in the sight block just ahead of the firer's eye. The firer has an excellent field of vision around the sight so that he can see what is happening around his target.

relation to the sight; there are no problems with parallax. Its precision may not suit a long range sniper, but for short ranges and fast shooting there is a lot to be said for this type of sight

With the advances of science during the Second World War it was not surprising that ways of defeating darkness were explored. Infra-red

devices were first thought of as a means of detecting targets at night by using an infra-red spotlight (which is invisible to the naked eye) together with a fairly simple low-power telescope capable of reacting to infra-red light. Since the infra-red filter on the spotlight absorbed a large amount of the light, the range of visibility was no more than two or three hundred yards, and the definition was not of the highest, but it was sufficient to detect moving figures. The drawback was that an enemy with a cheap and simple IR detector could see the light and take appropriate action.

Attaching this combination to a rifle was an obvious step, and British, American and German night-firing devices using an IR spotlight and sight were developed in the latter part of the war, though they saw little combat use.

After the war, interest languished until the 1960s introduced the transistor and miniaturised electronic circuitry. By this time, too, there had been renewed interest in infra-red as a method of guiding missiles and IR detectors had been significantly improved. By borrowing some techniques from the IR field and inventing new ones in the electronics field, it suddenly became possible to place an image of the target on to a luminescent screen and then electronically amplify the contrast between the millions of elements making up this screen so that what began as a dim view ended up as a bright picture. Provided there was some light on the scene to begin with,

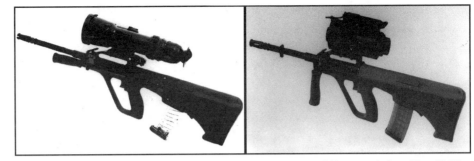

A typical first-generation Image Intensifying sight, the StarTron, mounted on an Austrian AUG assault rifle.

Same rifle, different sight. The Philips UV1137 second-generation self-powered sight on the AUG rifle, half the size and about two-thirds of the weight of the StarTron.

amplification of ten or twenty thousand times would produce a recognisable image. Once more this began as a tool of observation, but it was soon adapted as a weapon sight, the 'Image Intensifying' (II) sight. These 'First Generation' II sights were usually about 12-16 inches (300-400mm) long and weighed between 4 and 6 lbs (2-3kg), and carrying a rifle with one of those clamped on top of it was no joke. Aiming was not easy, either, because the weight above the rifle tended to make it cant to one side unless the firer was able to rest the weapon on something. They were also gluttons for batteries and some of them emitted a supersonic whine which

tended to upset wild or domestic animals within earshot, to the embarrassment of the would-be clandestine sniper. But for all that they proved to be a revelation to the night-fighting soldier, giving him a bright and recognisable image of his target out to three or four hundred yards range.

These large First Generation sights were replaced by the smaller Second Generation types in the early 1980s. These used a different technology to amplify the light, using less power and compressing the mystery into a smaller space, so that rifle sights suddenly became half the size and half the weight. They also gave a better

Above: The Russian PGN-1 first generation night sight on an RPK-74 machine gun.
Right: The Israeli Elop Mini night weapon sight on an M16 rifle.

picture and were more resistant to flashes (which tended to blank out the first generation tubes for several seconds) and also to shocks and strains. Finally, in the late 1980s came the Third Generation, which was the same circuitry but with a more sensitive image screen which could provide more detail and thus give a better picture, and also produced a stronger electrical impulse which permitted easier amplification.

Meanwhile, infra-red had made a sensational comeback. Largely as a method of aerial reconnaissance, 'Thermal Imaging' (TI) had been perfected. This means that instead of flooding the area with IR light, the detector now sets out to detect the difference in temperature of the myriad of things it sees. A difference of as little as 0.5°C can be detected at long ranges and every change in temperature brings about a different shade of grey in the picture displayed. Since everything has some definite temperature, and since different substances absorb the sun's heat and reflect it at different values, at any given moment the various items on the face of the earth - houses, cars, tanks, men, trees - all have a subtly different temperature, and a sensitive detector can produce a picture almost as good as a photograph. This sort of apparatus originally filled a large aircraft, but it was gradually refined and refined until we now have Thermal Imagers which can fit on top of a rifle and which can be sensitive enough to reveal a man at several hundred yards range.

Moreover, TI has the advantage of being able to 'see' through screens. A man standing behind a bush will be invisible to the naked eye, or to a telescope or even to an II sight. But the TI sight will detect the heat behind the bush and, if it does not actually outline the man, will certainly say "There's something behind that bush!".

An early version of the US Army's Short Range Thermal Sight made by Honeywell. This uses an uncooled 'Ambient Temperature Imaging Module' thus doing away with one of the greatest problems facing thermal sight developers: the need to keep the detector at well below 0° C to make it work.

The most recent advances in this quarter, still under development, involve viewing the same scene through TI and II sights and mixing the two images to produce what is called a 'gray-fused' picture in which more detail is visible than in either of the two individual sources. For reasons which we need not pursue, the two sources also provide pictures at different frequencies, and some highly scientific technology can be applied to these so that 'pseudo-colour' can result, giving the firer a coloured picture which, if not entirely true to life, certainly accentuates the difference between houses, trees, vehicles and so forth. However, at the present time this sort of technology is strictly laboratory stuff; it is unlikely to appear on any weapon for at least ten years.

Having got the weapon and the sight, the next stage is to adjust the sight so that the bullet arrives where the sight is pointed; the process known as 'zeroing' the rifle. The one fact to bear in mind here is that the bullet does not travel in a straight line from the muzzle to the target. Air resistance slows it and gravity pulls it, so that the shape of its flight - or trajectory - is a gentle curve. So to hit a target 400 yards away, the muzzle has to be lifted up so that the curving path of the bullet lands at 400 yards. What this means is that the rifle has to be zeroed - the sight and the trajectory brought into coincidence - at some specific range. The adjustment of the sight is calculated for the specific ammunition in use, so that once a definite relationship has been established at one range, adjusting

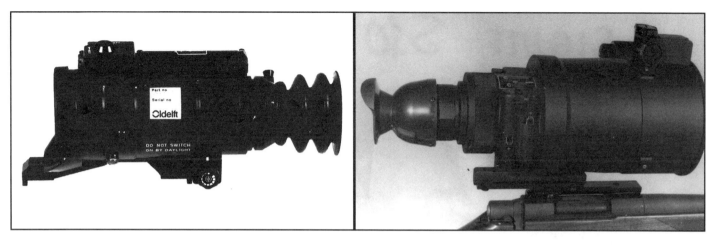

Above: From the Netherlands: the Oldelft MS4GT rifle sight. It weighs just 1kg (2.2lbs) and is 260mm (10.2in) long. has 4x magnification and runs on two AA batteries.

Above right: The American StarTron Mark 500 Multi-Mission riflescope. A second-generation instrument, it can be fitted with any number of different object lenses to give fields of view and magnification suited to different tasks and weapons. With a 100mm f/1.7 lens it is compact enough for assault rifles, but fitting a 170mm f/1.5 lens boosts the magnification to 9.5x and is well suited to sniping duties.

the sight to other ranges will automatically bring the bullet on to the aiming point. Zeroing used to be a long and tedious business which demanded a firing range and, often, an armourer. The soldier, with his new rifle, would fire a group of shots at a specified range. The armourer would examine the placing of the shots relative to the aiming mark and then adjust the sights. He might even change the foresight for a lower or higher one, reset the sight
to one side or another, reset the rear sights and so on until, after more trial groups, the bullets were ringed around

the aiming point. The rifle was then zeroed for that man at that range. A few trial shots at other ranges would then confirm the zero and that was that. Once this initial zeroing was completed, subsequent zeroing was in the nature of a check, with minor, if any, adjustments. But it still demanded a firing range, ammunition, and time.

Zeroing can still be done this way, and it is probable that most snipers will do it at frequent intervals. But there are times when zeroing by shooting is not possible. For example, a sniper is rushed to a hostage situation; he hasn't fired the rifle for some time, it may have

Above: An early British first-generation sight was this Pullin SS-84, seen here on a Parker-Hale Model 85 rifle.

Left: For rifles already fitted with an optical sight, like the Steyr AUG, the Simrad KN250 night sight from Norway can be fitted on top of the telescope and coupled to it by a prism in front of the telescope object lens. The KN250 produces a picture of the scene in starlight or moonlight, and this picture can then be viewed through the rifle telescope in the ordinary way. Since the zeroing is unaffected, provided the firer takes aim correctly on the picture he sees, his shot will strike the right place.

Above: The Signaal-Usfa UA 1137 night sight is a very versatile instrument. With a 22° horizontal field of view, it makes a good surveillance and observation scope when held in the hand. The vertical field of 10° ensures that the user is shielded from sky illumination and from the flash of his rifle. Fitted to a rifle it is a compact and effective sight. But the most unusual feature is that it does not require batteries. A quick (and silent) depression of the lever lying along the top of the sight charges it up by means of a condenser circuit. Five to ten strokes is enough to power it for an hour or more.

Above: Another dry zero device, this time mounted into the barrel of an SA80 rifle and aligned with the optical sight. The firer now looks through his sight at the grid which he sees in the lens of the device and records the coordinates of his crosswires. All he has to do to check his zero is to put the device back in to the muzzle and look through his sight to check whether his crosswires are aligned on the correct coordinates.

Right: A pair of dry zeroing devices, mounted on their 'spuds' - carefully dimensioned rods which fit precisely into the rifle barrel.

been knocked, he has no guarantee that it is still in zero. He can't check by firing because he is already at the site of the action. What does he do?

He uses a 'dry zero' device. This is an optical device which can be used to establish the axis of the rifle bore

and its relationship to the axis of the sight. It consists of a short optical unit mounted on a bracket which is fixed to a 'spud' or rod of the correct diameter for the calibre of the particular weapon in use. Once the device is adopted, the weapon is taken

out to a range and zeroed in the traditional manner. Once the sights have been adjusted to the firer's satisfaction, the dry zero instrument spud is inserted into the bore so that the instrument sits above the barrel and lies in the sight line. The firer then looks through his sight and sees a gridded screen in the lens of the device. He can now make a note of the precise position on the

136

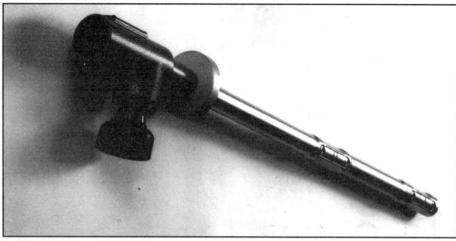

Left: Another way of dry zeroing. The device in the muzzle of the rifle is a telescope directed at the distant screen. On the left is an eyepiece through which the pointing of the rifle barrel can be directed. After the rifle has been aligned with the screen, the sights can be adjusted to the correct point of alignment with the barrel,

Above: *The front view of the telescope dry zero device.*

screen, by means of numbered co-ordinates like a map, of the crosswires of his telescope or other aiming mark of his sight. Once this is recorded, the initial work is done.

Now, when he arrives at the hostage scene with his rifle, he also carries his dry-zero instrument. He simply lies down in a convenient spot, puts the instrument into the bore, looks through his sight and checks that the crosswires still line up with his set of coordinates. If not, he adjusts his sight until they do, after which he knows that the sight is at its original zero.

Another system is simply to mount a right-angled telescope on the end of the spud so that when inserted into the barrel the telescope is in prolongation of the axis of the bore. After zeroing in the normal way, the instrument is inserted and the rifle aimed at a graduated screen, the telescope being carefully laid on the centre mark. The position of the sight is then checked, coordinates recorded, and that's that. Checking in the future is simply a matter of putting up the screen, fitting the telescope into the bore, laying the scope on the centre and checking where the sight line lies, adjusting it if necessary. A variation of this system is to have a laser spotlight on the end of the spud and use this to lay on the centre of the graduated screen.

Sniping is an art, not a science; that is because the instant that the bullet leaves the rifle the sniper has no further control over events. The sniper's art lies in being able to forecast what is going to happen in that space between the muzzle and the target, and in making adjustments and allowances for it before he fires. And the two things which are the principal hurdles are range and cross-wind.

Cross-wind he can do little about except watch for clues in the way that trees and bushes bend, how grass waves, how smoke and dust move. Range was more or less in the same class until twenty years ago; a man who could estimate range with any degree of accuracy was a valuable property. Some telescopes had crosswires marked off vertically so that a standing man could be fitted in between one lower fixed mark and one of a number of higher marks, and according to which mark his head reached, you could read off the range. It was a fairly reasonable system but it

A British Army sniper with his L96A1 rifle, aiming by means of a Pilkington 'Maxi-Kite' night sight. Maxi-Kite has 6x magnification, a 5.5° field of view, and provides a high-resolution image for aiming. It is 360mm (14in) long, weighs 1.5kg (3lbs) and is powered by two AA batteries. The user can recognise a standing man at 450 metres distance in starlight.

relied upon two things - a six-foot soldier, and a soldier standing to attention. And for some reason or other, six-foot soldiers standing upright are thin on the ground in war.

Optical rangefinders were available, but optical rangefinders tend to be bulky and heavy. The Barr & Stroud which formed part of the infantry machine gun section's tools was three

feet long, weighed about 20 lbs in the morning and about half-a-ton by evening (or so it felt) and, provided it was carefully handled and frequently checked, gave an answer which was within the accuracy of a rifle or machine gun.

Optical rangefinders are still available; the picture on the next page shows one, which is capable of being

LORIS (Laser Optical Rangefinding System) has a laser rangefinder incorporated into the casing of a telescope sight. The range is displayed in the telescope eyepiece and the firer then adjusts his telescope accordingly.

transformed into a periscope for peering around cover. There is something to be said for one of these instruments - at least they don't run out of power at an inopportune moment, and they give stereoscopic vision, which can be very useful at times - but it has to be said that they can be something of a burden.

Though one would not say that if the laser rangefinder had not been invented; this is the device which has virtually made optical rangefinding obsolete. A small device no larger than a pair of binoculars, and somewhat lighter in most cases, it will measure range in a split second and deliver an answer accurate to five metres up to as far as any rifle can shoot. The only cloud on the horizon is the growing appearance of laser detectors; these are actually designed to warn against laser designators which might be in use to direct a missile or smart munition towards the enemy, but if a detector is scanning the area it could react to a rangefinder signal and cause something of an alarm. Whether it could identify the signal as coming from a rangefinder is another question.

In tank gunnery, which some might consider to be sniping on a grand scale, the laser rangefinder has been integrated into the sighting system, so that as the gunner lays his sight upon the target the laser rangefinder is automatically aligned. A computer, primed with the characteristics - muzzle velocity, weight, ballistic coefficient and so forth - of the projectile, and kept up to date on such matters as wind speed, temperature and degree of dislevelment of the tank itself, is also coupled into the system. When the gunner has selected his target he presses a button; the laser finds the range and tells the computer,

The Bofors A40P periscopic rangefinder in use. The design is unusual in that the viewer is at one end of the instrument, rather than in the middle which is more usual with rangefinders. But building it this way means that the user can remain concealed and protected whilst taking the range or viewing the scenery. It can also be turned vertically and used from a fox-hole or from behind a wall.

Much neater and lighter than an optical rangefinder is this Zeiss 'Halem' laser rangefinder, weighing 2.5kg (5.5lbs) and only 200mm (7.8in) wide. It will measure ranges from 50 metres to 2 kilometres with an accuracy of 5 metres.

Right: The first successful laser/computer/telescope combination was 'CLASS' (Computerised Laser Sighting System) developed in Canada. Some idea of its size can be gathered from this picture which shows it in use on an 84mm Carl Gustav anti-tank gun. It produces the complete ballistic solution and re-aligns the telescope crosswires. There is obviously some more work to be done before this system can be applied to a rifle.

which then performs prodigies of mathematics and ends up by moving the telescope crosswires in the field of view. The gunner re-lays his crosswires on to the target, and in doing so has aimed off the necessary amount to compensate for wind, drift, temperature and every other correctable variable known to man. He fires and hits.

Once this system became general knowledge, it was simply a matter of time before somebody thought of applying it to a rifle. But whilst you can hang all sorts of temperature and wind sensors on a tank, you cannot do it on a rifle, so a lot of the computing goes out of the window. What is left is the basic ballistics of the bullet - muzzle velocity, drift, coefficient, weight -

Above: This was TeleRanger, the first laser/telescope combination. Developed in Austria, the laser simply attached to the telescope. After switching the unit on, the sniper could press the button, on the side of the rifle below the telescope object lens, to take a range. He then read the range from a display above the telescope eyepiece and adjusted his telescope.

a simple pre-programmed microchip can deal with those. Couple a laser rangefinder to the telescope, put the microchip in there somewhere, arrange some mechanism for displacing the crosswires, and the job is done. It sounds easy, but putting everything into a convenient shape, size and weight to go on top of a rifle and withstand the firing shock took a year or two. What came first was LORIS - the Laser Optical Rangefinding Sight - and TeleRanger. These were conventional telescope sights with laser rangefinders attached or built in. A simple pressure switch could be taped to any convenient part of the rifle so that as the firer began to take aim she could press the switch and the laser fired and then displayed the range in the telescope field of view. Indeed the speed of the laser is such that it can take three measurements, calculate the mean range and display it within a couple of seconds, so that the firer can then adjust his range drum accordingly.

At the present moment, apart from some experimental equipments, there is no computing laser sight for a sniping rifle. They have been developed for crew-served weapons such as heavy machine guns and recoilless guns, but their weight and bulk puts them out of court for rifle use. Moreover, there is a viewpoint which suggests that this is really gilding the lily. So long as the firer has an accurate range, that's all he needs, and since the computer can do no more than adjust the crosswires to the required range, one is liable to end up paying a very large sum of money for something which can be done by the simple combination of laser and telescope described above. Full ballistic compensation might be worth it, but the array of sensors and gadgets required to attain that goal would be totally impractical.

MALOS is the Israeli computing sight. This contains a laser rangefinder, telescope and computing chip programmed for the ammunition in use. An operating button located anywhere on the weapon can be used to fire the laser, after which the range is passed to the chip and an aiming mark is displayed in the field of view at the appropriate point. Seen here mounted on an anti-tank rocket launcher, MALOS weighs only 1.2kg (2.6lbs), is 350mm (13.75in) long, and has been successfully tested on a rifle.

GLOSSARY

Anti-Materiel Rifle
A heavy-calibre rifle intended for long range attack on vulnerable high-technology targets such as communications centres, radar sets, parked aircraft or fuel dumps.

Box Magazine
A form of ammunition supply in which the cartridges are contained in a metal box, either detachable from the weapon or forming an integral part of it, and are pushed towards the mouth of the magazine by a spring so as to enter the feedway of the weapon.

Bullpup
A rifle in which the breech mechanism is set back in the stock so that the rear of the receiver is against the firer's shoulder. It permits the use of a full-length barrel in a weapon which is, overall, shorter than a conventionally-stocked weapon of the same barrel length.

Calibre
The internal diameter of a weapon barrel, measured across the 'lands', the ungrooved sectors of the bore.

Drift
The sideways movement of the bullet during its flight, cause by the spin imparted to it by the weapon's rifling. The sight is usually designed to provide an average compensation for drift at the usual range over the weapon's employment, but additional adjustment may be required at long ranges.

EOD
Explosive Ordnance Disposal; the disposal, by rendering safe or by destruction, of an explosive munition or device.

Feedway
That part of a firearm in which the cartridge is placed, either by hand or by the magazine system, so as to be loaded into the chamber.

Gas Operation
A method of operating an automatic or semi-automatic weapon by diverting some of the propelling gas behind the bullet into a cylinder where it drives a piston. This piston is connected to the weapon's bolt and, under gas pressure, extracts the empty case and loads a fresh round. Alternatively, the gas can be channelled so as to strike the bolt or bolt carrier directly and thus move it.

Graticule
The cross-wires or other aiming mark in the field of view of a telescope sight.

Image Intensification
Electronic enhancement of a dimly-lit scene viewed through an optical sight; the minute differences in the strength of the light on the different parts of the target are electronically amplified until the picture is sufficiently distinct for recognition of the target and weapon aiming.

MPI
Mean Point of Impact. The mathematical centre of a group of shots (usually five or ten) fired at the same point of aim.

Recoil Operation
Method of operating an automatic or semi-automatic weapon by making use of the force of recoil due to firing a bullet from the barrel. The barrel recoils under this force, and this movement can be used to reload the weapon.

Reticle
A form of graticule (see above) which incorporates markers which are a specified distance apart and can thus be used as a range-finding aid. The word is, wrongly, often used interchangeably with 'graticule'.

Sub-sonic
Below the speed of sound. Sound travels at 1118 feet per second (340 metres/sec) at sea level, and an object (such as a bullet) moving at a greater speed generates a sound-wave (the 'sonic bang'). Thus a weapon which is silenced must fire sub-sonic ammunition, otherwise the noise of the bullet will reveal its presence.

Thermal Imaging
The detection of minute temperature differences at the target and the electronic translation of these temperature differences into a coherent picture, allowing recognition of the target and aiming of the weapon.

Velocity
The speed of the bullet, usually given in feet or metres per second. It defined as 'Muzzle Velocity' when speaking of the speed at which the bullet leaves the weapon; 'Observed Velocity', the speed at any particular point during its flight; or 'Terminal Velocity', the speed at which it strikes the target.

Windage
The lateral adjustment of a weapon sight to compensate for the sideways movement of the bullet during flight due to the effects of wind.

Zeroing
The act of adjusting the sights of a weapon so that the point of aim and the MPI (see above) are in the same place on the target. Zeroing is carried out at one specific range, and the weapon sight is designed so that at other ranges the correct relationship is maintained.